D0531903

German infanterymen, under shellfire during the
blitzkrieg, dash through a village whose road
sign shows they have just entered France. Fast-
moving foot soldiers like these were part of
the new concept of war in which mobile infantry
exploited gains made by tanks and aircraft.

BLITZKRIEG

Other Publications:
LIBRARY OF HEALTH
CLASSICS OF THE OLD WEST
THE EPIC OF FLIGHT
THE GOOD COOK
THE SEAFARERS
THE ENCYCLOPEDIA OF COLLECTIBLES
THE GREAT CITIES
HOME REPAIR AND IMPROVEMENT
THE WORLD'S WILD PLACES
THE TIME-LIFE LIBRARY OF BOATING
HUMAN BEHAVIOR
THE ART OF SEWING
THE OLD WEST
THE EMERGENCE OF MAN
THE AMERICAN WILDERNESS
THE TIME-LIFE ENCYCLOPEDIA OF GARDENING
LIFE LIBRARY OF PHOTOGRAPHY
THIS FABULOUS CENTURY
FOODS OF THE WORLD
TIME-LIFE LIBRARY OF AMERICA
TIME-LIFE LIBRARY OF ART
GREAT AGES OF MAN
LIFE SCIENCE LIBRARY
THE LIFE HISTORY OF THE UNITED STATES
TIME READING PROGRAM
LIFE NATURE LIBRARY
LIFE WORLD LIBRARY
FAMILY LIBRARY:
  HOW THINGS WORK IN YOUR HOME
  THE TIME-LIFE BOOK OF THE FAMILY CAR
  THE TIME-LIFE FAMILY LEGAL GUIDE
  THE TIME-LIFE BOOK OF FAMILY FINANCE

This volume is one of a series that chronicles in
full the events of the Second World War. The
previous book in the series is:

Prelude to War

WORLD WAR II · TIME-LIFE BOOKS · ALEXANDRIA, VIRGINIA

BY ROBERT WERNICK
AND THE EDITORS OF TIME-LIFE BOOKS

BLITZKRIEG

Time-Life Books Inc.
is a wholly owned subsidiary of
TIME INCORPORATED

Founder: Henry R. Luce 1898-1967

Editor-in-Chief: Henry Anatole Grunwald
President: J. Richard Munro
Chairman of the Board: Ralph P. Davidson
Executive Vice President: Clifford J. Grum
Chairman, Executive Committee: James R. Shepley
Editorial Director: Ralph Graves
Group Vice President, Books: Joan D. Manley
Vice Chairman: Arthur Temple

TIME-LIFE BOOKS INC.

Managing Editor: Jerry Korn
Executive Editor: David Maness
Assistant Managing Editors: Dale M. Brown
(planning), George Constable, Martin Mann,
John Paul Porter, Gerry Schremp (acting)
Art Director: Tom Suzuki
Chief of Research: David L. Harrison
Director of Photography: Robert G. Mason
Assistant Art Director: Arnold C. Holeywell
Assistant Chief of Research: Carolyn L. Sackett
Assistant Director of Photography: Dolores A. Littles

Chairman: John D. McSweeney
President: Carl G. Jaeger
Executive Vice Presidents: John Steven Maxwell,
David J. Walsh
Vice Presidents: George Artandi (comptroller);
Stephen L. Bair (legal counsel); Peter G. Barnes;
Nicholas Benton (public relations);
John L. Canova; Beatrice T. Dobie (personnel);
Carol Flaumenhaft (consumer affairs);
James L. Mercer (Europe/South Pacific);
Herbert Sorkin (production); Paul R. Stewart
(marketing)

WORLD WAR II

Editorial Staff for *Blitzkrieg*
Editor: Charles Osborne
Picture Editor/Designer: Charles Nikolaycak
Text Editor: Valerie Moolman
Staff Writers: Ruth Kelton, James Randall
Researchers: Josephine Reidy, Josephine G. Burke,
Doris Coffin, Henry Wiencek
Editorial Assistant: Cecily Gemmell

Editorial Production
Production Editor: Feliciano Madrid
Operations Manager: Gennaro C. Esposito,
Gordon E. Buck (assistant)
Quality Control: Robert L. Young (director),
James J. Cox (assistant), Daniel J. McSweeney,
Michael G. Wight (associates)
Art Coordinator: Anne B. Landry
Copy Staff: Susan B. Galloway (chief),
Mary Ellen Slate, Celia Beattie
Picture Department: Martin Baldessari
Traffic: Kimberly K. Lewis

Correspondents: Elisabeth Kraemer (Bonn);
Margot Hapgood, Dorothy Bacon, Lesley Coleman
(London); Susan Jonas, Lucy T. Voulgaris (New
York); Maria Vincenza Aloisi, Josephine du Brusle
(Paris); Ann Natanson (Rome). Valuable assistance
was also provided by: Judy Aspinall (London);
Carolyn T. Chubet, Miriam Hsia, Christina
Lieberman (New York); Mimi Murphy (Rome).

The Author: ROBERT WERNICK, a former staff member of *Life*, is a freelance writer with a long-standing interest in the European campaigns of World War II. He is the author of *The Monument Builders* in The Emergence of Man series and *The Vikings* in The Seafarers series. He has published several novels, and written many articles on subjects that range from art to psychology.

The Consultants: A. E. CAMPBELL is Professor of American History at the University of Birmingham, England. He was formerly Fellow and Tutor of Modern History at Keble College, Oxford, and has been Visiting Professor at several American universities. He is the author of *Great Britain and the United States: 1895-1903*.

COLONEL JOHN R. ELTING, USA (Ret.), is a military historian and author of *The Battle of Bunker's Hill*, *The Battles of Saratoga* and *Military History and Atlas of the Napoleonic Wars*. He edited *Military Uniforms in America: The Era of the American Revolution, 1755-1795* and *Military Uniforms of America: Years of Growth, 1796-1851*, and was associate editor of *The West Point Atlas of American Wars*.

HANS-ADOLF JACOBSEN, Director of the Seminar for Political Science at the University of Bonn, is the co-author of *Anatomy of the S.S.*, and editor of *Decisive Battles of World War II: The German View*.

HENRI MICHEL, an officer of the Legion of Honor, is president of both the French National Committee and the International Committee for the History of the Second World War. His book *The Second World War* won the French Academy's Prix Gobert in 1970.

JAMES P. SHENTON, Professor of History at Columbia University, has lectured frequently on educational television. He is the author of *History of the United States from 1865 to the Present* and *Robert John Walker: A Politician from Jackson to Lincoln*.

Library of Congress Cataloguing in Publication Data

Wernick, Robert, 1918-
  Blitzkrieg.

    (World War II; v. 2)
    Bibliography: p. 204
    Includes index.
    1. World War, 1939-1945—Campaigns.
  I. Time-Life Books.   II. Title.   III. Series.
  D743.W44   940.53   76-25750
  ISBN 0-8094-2456-8
  ISBN 0-8094-2455-X (lib. bdg.)
  ISBN 0-8094-2454-1 (retail ed.)

For information about any Time-Life book, please write:

Reader Information
Time-Life Books
541 North Fairbanks Court
Chicago, Illinois 60611

CONTENTS

AN EPOCHAL WEEKEN

A Berlin taxi driver, a garage attendant and a nattily dressed youth salute Hitler's speech announcing war against Poland, broadcast over street loudspeakers.

FACING UP TO THE HOLIDAY'S END

On Friday, September 1, 1939, the sound of German artillery aimed at Polish defenders along the Vistula River echoed only faintly at first in the capitals of Western Europe. As Hitler announced the war to the Reichstag and the German nation at 10 o'clock that morning there were no bands, no marching soldiers, no cheering masses in Berlin. No crowds descended upon government buildings in London to demonstrate sympathy for Poland. In Paris, the reaction of the average Frenchman was a Gallic shrug and a resigned "Let's get it over with."

For two days life went on in the major cities of Europe as if the war were a thousand miles away. Europeans gave up their last days of warmth and peace reluctantly: Berliners drank chocolate and sipped schnapps on sun-filled café terraces; Frenchmen enjoyed an afternoon swim or a movie matinee; and Britons savored the bittersweet pleasures of a late summer holiday.

Still, war's reality could not be ignored. Antiaircraft barrage balloons floated over London from Friday noon on. Sandbags bolstered walls and stairways. Women and children began to trickle out of the city to the safety of the countryside. In Paris evacuation notices went up in the squares, and seriously ill hospital patients, their beds needed for war casualties, were bundled into trucks and buses for the journey to areas deemed safer than the capital. Reluctant civilian soldiers donned uniforms and headed for their units as France called for general mobilization of reserves, and the British wrote conscription into their laws.

Finally, on Sunday, September 3, at 11:15 a.m., the BBC broadcast Prime Minister Neville Chamberlain's brief announcement that "This country is at war with Germany." Within minutes of his speech, Londoners experienced their first wartime air-raid alert; in Paris and Berlin sirens sounded later the same day, and the citizens of all three cities took to their shelters.

That Sunday the alarms were false; no bombs dropped anywhere in the West. But no one doubted that the summer was over, and that war had begun.

London shoppers and businessmen read Friday morning's news: Germany had invaded Poland before dawn; Parliament would convene at 6 p.m.

Strollers near the Paris Opéra check a large notice board for evacuation routes to areas outside the city. At least two prudently carry their gas masks.

This cheerful sign on a luggage-laden British car expresses the determination of one Englishman not to allow the outbreak of World War II to spoil his holiday.

On the sidewalks and café terraces lining
Paris' Champs Elysées, Saturday boulevardiers
take their customary stroll and apéritif,
while only a few blocks away at the Elysée
Palace France's ministers prepare the
next day's declaration of war on Germany.

A young Luftwaffe brigadier general reads the
news of the War's first weekend at a Berlin
café table. In the early days of the conflict, the
relatively few uniformed men to be seen
in the cities were lionized as national heroes.

French reservists (right) read the order for general mobilization, which has just been posted. Members of the army reserve were to report to their units on Saturday, September 2. In England, where some reserve troops had already been called up in late August, the weekend newspapers (above) announce the National Service Act calling for a draft of "all fit men 18 to 41" into the armed forces. In both countries, anti-Nazi volunteers of many different nationalities were already crowding recruiting offices.

Patients and nurses gather in the courtyard
of the Saint-Antoine Hospital—a major blood-
transfusion center—where buses and
ambulances wait to take them out of Paris.
Over 3,000 invalids were evacuated from
the city in a single afternoon during the first
few days of the War, freeing beds for an
avalanche of wounded that never materialized.

Two London businessmen, equipped with the
gas masks obligatory in Britain, stop for a
chat in the heart of the financial district. Behind
them sandbags buttress an ancient wall, and a
portable canvas reservoir stands ready to supply
the London Auxiliary Fire Service with a reserve
source of water in case of incendiary bombing.

Under the supervision of a policeman, a volunteer in Berlin kneels on sandbags to post an air-raid shelter sign in a shop window.

15

As one man scans the sky apprehensively for signs of German planes, the sound of air-raid sirens sends Sunday strollers and shoppers scurrying along a rainy Paris street to the nearest bomb shelter. When the all-clear sounded, Parisians climbed out of steamy cellars and Metro stations into a city that was still untouched by German bombs.

1

On August 17, 1939, General Franz Halder, chief of staff of the German Army, noted in his diary a rather odd request from Heinrich Himmler, chief of Hitler's Schutzstaffeln—or protection squads—the Nazi Party's own armed forces. Himmler wanted a supply of Polish military uniforms. The German Army performed with its customary efficiency. The uniforms were requisitioned, procured, delivered.

Very probably, neither Halder nor any other Army commander was aware that the clothing was an essential element in a scheme by which Hitler planned to establish a pretext for an all-out attack on Poland. Some time between the August 17 entry in Halder's diary and August 31—the eve of the attack—13 convicted criminals were taken from a concentration camp at Oranienburg in eastern Germany and installed in a nearby schoolhouse, where they were to be held until the scheme was ripe.

Code-named "Operation Canned Goods"—it was the German convicts who were the goods—the project had two phases. On August 31, in the first stage, all but one of the prisoners were ordered to dress themselves in the Polish uniforms; then they were given fatal injections of a drug, and taken to a small forest near Hochlinde, about 10 miles west of the German-Polish border, where they were shot. Their bodies were arranged to make it appear that they had died while advancing into Germany; foreign journalists and other witnesses were subsequently brought to the scene to view the evidence of the corpses.

Later the same day, in the second phase of Operation Canned Goods, the remaining prisoner, escorted by Major Alfred Naujocks and five other members of the SS security branch (the SD), was hustled off to the nearby town of Gleiwitz; the party, all wearing civilian clothes, burst into the local radio station and took it over. One of Naujocks' colleagues, speaking in Polish, broadcast an inflammatory statement announcing that Poland was attacking Germany, and calling all Poles to join the colors. Then, after a simulated scuffle between the disguised SD men and the station personnel that involved much confusion and a good deal of shooting in front of an open microphone, the civilian-clad prisoner was killed and left lying on the studio floor—to impersonate the firebrand "Polish" broadcaster.

The next day at 10 a.m., in a speech before the Reichstag in Berlin, Adolf Hitler cited the charade at Gleiwitz as an in-

HITLER WEATHER

stance of Polish aggression on German soil, and announced that he had thrown all the armed might of Germany against the attacking nation.

Thus he launched World War II.

This was, in many important ways, Hitler's own war, started at the time and the place of his choice. After six years of spectacular bloodless triumphs over enemies both domestic and foreign—his assumption of power, the rearmament of Germany, the reoccupation of the Rhineland, the union forced upon Austria, the seizure of Czechoslovakia—the time had now come for the Führer to prove himself as a warlord on the field of battle.

On April 3, Hitler had issued written orders to his High Command for the attack on Poland, the operation to commence any time after September 1. On May 23, he had lectured his top officers for hours on the subject of his plans. He said he was burning his bridges; the solution of Germany's problems—arising, as Hitler saw them, from the need for expanded living space for the people of the Reich—was unattainable "without invading other countries or attacking other people's possessions."

Hitler went on: "Further successes are impossible without the shedding of blood." And that first blood was to be shed in Poland.

In his newly declared quest after military victory, Hitler's chief weapon, complementing his grasp of such political stratagems as secrecy, bluff and deception, was a form of swift, mechanized, mobile warfare that the world had never before seen. The total concept was called blitzkrieg, or lightning war, in which coordinated forces of armored (panzer) divisions, high-level bombers, dive bombers and motorized infantry divisions would smash through enemy defenses in a sudden, massive assault.

The generals in the Führer's captive audience may well have squirmed when he summarized the risks of his belligerent policy: the strong possibility existed of intervention by Britain and France, with the Soviet Union threatening from the east. But few of the officers voiced doubts or even asked questions, although they all were aware that the German war machine had neither the military muscle nor the industrial depth to win a war against all those potential enemies. Fearful of the dictator, swayed by his success to date, they now defined themselves as obedient tools of his

will. Most also had a mystical faith that he could limit the war, could take on his enemies piecemeal and—above all—could prevent the Soviet Union from forming an effective alliance with the Western democracies that would force the Germans into the nightmare of a two-front war.

In the weeks following the May meeting, Hitler was able to bring off all these feats, and the generals' faith in his magic was upheld. Perhaps the most important of the Führer's accomplishments had been the signing of the crucial Nazi-Soviet nonaggression pact on August 23 (a scant week before the German assault on Poland), which not only guaranteed to Germany a free hand in the east but also assured a secure rear in case of operations in the west. Stalin, in return, obtained a franchise on spheres of influence in eastern Poland, in parts of southeastern Europe, in Finland and in the Baltic states of Latvia and Estonia—from the German viewpoint, a small price to pay for Russian cooperation.

Therefore it was with supreme confidence in himself, his intuition and his guiding star that Hitler rose before the obedient brown-shirted Reichstag deputies on the morning of September 1, and told them that he had put on the field-gray uniform of the German soldier, the "sacred coat" he had worn in the trenches of World War I, and would not take it off short of victory or death. By then, the first phase of his military campaign against the Poles had already begun. In the darkness before dawn, almost six hours earlier, an assault by land, sea and air had been launched and every sign pointed to a quick German victory.

The first shots were fired at Danzig in the Polish Corridor, which cut East Prussia off from the Reich. Polish control of the old Hanseatic port had long been a source of resentment to the Germans, and Hitler saw a symbolic value in its repossession on the first day of war.

A couple of days earlier the *Schleswig-Holstein*, a training ship of the German Navy, had steamed into the harbor of Danzig on what was announced as a courtesy visit. But the crew had a more urgent mission than to go sightseeing among the picturesque gabled houses of the medieval merchant-princes of Danzig. Though the *Schleswig-Holstein* was a relic of a battleship, built in 1906, it was still a battleship, armed with powerful 11-inch guns. On the morning of September 1, it turned these guns against the Polish fortress of

Westerplatte, which guarded Danzig's harbor. The garrison had no comparable armament, and could only submit grimly to a steady, murderous bombardment.

Meanwhile, as day broke on the land frontier, Polish General Wladyslaw Anders, commanding a division stationed at the village of Lidzbark, 90 miles southeast of Danzig and about 13 miles south of the East Prussian border, heard the sky fill with a menacing drone. In his memoirs Anders recalls how he and his men looked up to see squadron after squadron of German planes like flocks of cranes swooping south in the direction of Warsaw.

These were Hitler's high-level bombers. In the course of a few hours they reduced much of the Polish rear to a shambles. They destroyed most of the Polish Air Force on the ground, blasting its planes, its hangars, its fuel dumps out of existence; they blew up railroad stations full of soldiers who were obeying their mobilization orders, savaged railroad trains, bridges, radio stations, headquarters buildings, barracks, and munitions factories. High-explosive and incendiary bombs set raging fires in the cities and panicked the civilian population.

Against the Polish defenders in the front lines near the border, the attack opened with waves of an unexpected and frightening weapon, the Junkers-87 dive bomber—the Stuka. The Stuka proved to be a fearsomely effective weapon, partially for psychological reasons. Many of these planes were fitted with sirens on their undercarriages; these sirens produced a screaming racket as the Stuka dived. And when it came plummeting down out of the sky with the ear-shattering sound of a great siren, every soldier on the ground thought that the dive bomber was aiming straight for him. Trained troops capable of withstanding an artillery bombardment of much greater destructiveness than the Stuka could deliver were demoralized—at least initially—by the sight and sound of this terror from the skies.

After the dive bombers came the motorcycles, the armored cars, the tanks—and after them the armored infantry and artillery of the panzer divisions, probing for soft spots in the Polish lines. When they found such weaknesses, they plunged through and fanned out in the rear, disrupting communications, bursting among formations of troops who had thought themselves secure miles behind the front, spreading confusion that easily turned to panic. Plunging forward

through open country, German mobile forces soon had the Polish armies split into fragments. Each of these broken pieces faced an impossible situation. In a sense, the harder they fought, the worse off they were. For if isolated units stood their ground and fought off frontal attacks on their positions, they would soon be surrounded by troops pouring through the gaps the panzers had made. On the other hand, if they retreated, they plunged into the hell that the blitzkrieg was generating in the rear.

Among civilians, the sudden descent of the planes and tanks, like so many beasts of the Apocalypse, spread disquieting news, then alarming rumors, then blind fear upon the peaceful hinterland. Householders rushed to throw some provisions and a few prized possessions onto farm wagons or wheelbarrows, or strapped them to their backs, and took to the roads—the very roads over which the Polish forces had to maneuver if they were to halt the onrushing German tides. Soon every highway and especially every

crossroad had become an inextricable confusion of desperate soldiers, frightened civilians, nervous horses and broken-down vehicles. And whenever the confusion had begun to straighten itself out, unopposed German planes could be counted on to return and to bomb and strafe tenuous order back to a chaos worse than before.

There was confusion on the German side as well. A unit of German infantry found a small plane circling above it and peppered the craft liberally with rifle fire until it landed in their midst; out stepped a raging Luftwaffe general in charge of ground-air coordination. In another part of the front, General Heinz Guderian, commanding the XIX Armored Corps, was speeding off to join his forward units in an armored car when his own artillery neatly bracketed him. Guderian's driver panicked and drove straight into a ditch, wrecking the car, and almost losing the German Army its greatest tank commander before he had had a chance to fight a battle. Guderian escaped without injury, found an-

other car and drove up to the Brahe River, which was still spanned by an intact bridge. But no German troops were manning the bridge; the local commander had decided that his men needed a rest. General Guderian himself had to rouse the men, tell them that securing the bridge was more important than a snooze and get them across the river in enough time to set up a defensive position and prevent the Polish forces from recapturing the span.

Guderian drove back to his headquarters at Zahn to find that his staff officers and clerks were hurriedly digging slit trenches and were setting up an antiaircraft gun. They were responding to a rumor that the Polish cavalry had broken through the German lines and was going to stick them all like pigs with their lances. Again, the general was forced to boot his men back to their work.

The Polish cavalry did turn up a couple of days later, but not at Guderian's headquarters. His swift advance had taken him from the German border clear across the Polish Corridor into East Prussia, cutting off sizable Polish forces to the north. Among these was the crack Pomorske Cavalry Brigade, which spearheaded an attempt to break out of the corridor and rejoin the main Polish forces to the southeast. As the Germans looked on in disbelief, the troopers came riding down from the north on splendid horses; white-gloved officers signaled the charge, trumpets sounded, pennons waved, sabers flashed in the sun. Like an animated page out of an old history book the brigade came forward across open fields, at a steady earth-shaking gallop, lances at the ready, straight into the fire of Guderian's tanks. In a few minutes the cavalry lay in a smoking, screaming mass of dismembered and disemboweled men and horses. When the survivors were trudging off to a German prison camp, some of them—according to one German account—were observed rapping incredulously on the sides of German tanks parked by the roadside: they had heard that the armor of the German tanks was made of cardboard.

Amidst such courageous folly as the charge of the Pomorske Brigade, and in spite of the occasional lapses by German units, the tank-led blitzkrieg forces slammed relentlessly through the Polish countryside. The weather blessed the invaders. September and October are frequently rainy months in these regions, and one substantial downpour

GRAND DESIGN FOR A WARRIOR'S DREAM

Every military man has dreamed of directing a classic battle in which his armies slash the enemy with the deadly precision prescribed by the arrows on his map. The map above of Hitler's blitzkrieg in Poland offers a rare picture of such a dream come true—though when Wehrmacht troops met Soviet forces *(lined arrows)* coming from the east, the triumphant panzers teetered momentarily on the nightmarish edge of the wrong war.

During the main battle against the Poles the Germans surged forward in set-piece order. After thrusting across the Polish border on September 1, one corps of the Third Army swept in on Warsaw, while another moved to trap fleeing Polish troops west of the city.

In the south, the Fourteenth Army roared through the city of Krakow, the Tenth Army shoved in between Lodz and Krakow, and other German units from Slovakia cut into the Polish rear and turned toward the Bug River. In the north, part of the Fourth Army raced through the Polish Corridor and invested Danzig; other Fourth Army units fanned out toward East Prussia, Warsaw and Kutno—where they linked with the Eighth Army to bag 170,000 Poles by mid-September.

As the near-perfect battle was ending, stunned German troops deep in Poland looked up to see Russian soldiers advancing. The High Command had not passed down word of a secret, high-level agreement calling for the Russian advance that began on September 17. In the melee when the powers met, sporadic gunfire killed and wounded a few German and Soviet soldiers before the two forces separated across a previously negotiated demarcation line along the Bug.

would have turned the dirt trails that formed much of Poland's primitive road system into bogs in which tanks, trucks and foot soldiers all might have bogged down.

But this September was different. Every night the Poles prayed for rain, and every day the sun came up relentlessly bright and red, baking the land to parade-ground hardness, allowing the motorized columns either to choose open roads or to go directly across country when the roads were blocked. Rivers, like the Vistula, that would have been formidable barriers in flood were now easily fordable in many places. People spoke of "Hitler weather" in the same way that, in the 17th Century they had spoken of "the Protestant wind" that blew William of Orange's fleet down the Channel for the last successful invasion of England while it kept Catholic King James's navy bottled up in the Thames.

Polish soldiers and refugees milling around on the parched land set up such huge clouds of dust that German Air Force observers could not form any idea of what was going on. The German High Command assumed that the main Polish forces had escaped eastward across the Vistula under all the dust, and directed General Gerd von Runstedt, Commander of the Eighth, Tenth and Fourteenth armies, to cross in his turn and follow them. However, Runstedt was convinced that they were still west of the river and after some argument got the orders changed. He was right: the biggest remaining effective Polish units were caught in a trap.

Hitler paid a visit to the battlefield on the fifth day of the campaign, and Guderian could point out to him proudly the traces of Polish defeat everywhere, the hundreds of guns destroyed or taken, the hundreds of square miles safely conquered, the thousands of prisoners, and all at a minuscule cost to his four divisions—150 dead and 700 wounded. Hitler recalled how the regiment in which he had served in World War I had been mowed down as it went over the top —2,000 casualties in a single day. He was more than ever sure that he had found the key to victory. Clearly, blitzkrieg worked; he had been vindicated. Indeed, a more balanced mind than Hitler's might well have been convinced that the stars in their courses were fighting for him.

In substance, blitzkrieg was an attempt to break out of the murderous pattern of stalemate and battles of attrition that had bled the nations of Europe in World War I. Both sides on the Western Front during that war had dreamed of a decisive breakthrough—a change from static combat to a campaign of movement. Often the long columns of infantry slogging up through the mud toward the trenches and the unending shell fire would see massed regiments of their own cavalry standing immobile and immaculate in the rear areas, waiting for the moment when they could gallop through a breach in the opposing trench line and wreak havoc upon the fleeing enemy. Millions of men died in the effort to make that hole in the line, but it was never big enough, and the cavalry never rode through.

The strictly military aspects of blitzkrieg, dependent upon large-scale deployment of armored forces with air support, contained nothing really new or specifically German. During the '20s and early '30s, such Western military theorists as General J. F. C. Fuller in England and Colonel Charles de Gaulle in France had worked out the theoretical battlefield possibilities of the all-out mechanized assault, basing their thinking on the few successful uses of tanks in World War I. But these inventive men were largely ignored in their own countries; their ideas were deemed heretical, even absurd. Fuller, an abrasive man who took the indifference to his ideas of his peers and superiors hard, had been eased out of the British Army, and de Gaulle, an equally outspoken soldier, was considered a crank. Only in Germany in the 1930s were bright young officers like Guderian, then a colonel, encouraged to experiment with the new ideas.

What General Guderian and his associates had proposed was that the cavalry be replaced with a mobile and less vulnerable front-line force of tracked and wheeled vehicles that could both make the initial attack and then achieve and exploit the breakthrough. They conceived the idea of "panzer divisions." These were self-contained organizations, each of which consisted typically of two tank regiments and a regiment of infantry and artillery. Associated smaller units—reconnaissance, combat engineer, antitank, antiaircraft, signal and service troops—were transported by either lightly armored half-tracked vehicles or trucks. Ideally, the bulk of the artillery was self-propelled.

Two or more of these panzer divisions would be grouped —often together with a motorized infantry division—into a panzer corps. Later, several such corps would be combined into panzer armies, which could operate independently behind the enemy's lines and completely disrupt his rear. These mechanized ground forces were to be supported by aircraft—long-range reconnaissance planes to spot targets and enemy troop movements, and fighters and dive bombers to provide a kind of aerial heavy artillery. Orthodox military opinion rejected these premises as foolhardy; traditionalists argued that despite air support, tanks roaming by themselves behind enemy lines would be like a herd of sheep that could be rounded up one by one before help could get to them from slower-moving infantry divisions.

In spite of the skepticism of his superiors, Guderian was given command of a motorized battalion in 1931 and permitted to carry out field exercises with armored cars and automobiles outfitted to look like tanks. Fortunately for him, he was soon to have one highly unorthodox superior—Adolf Hitler. At the first military maneuvers he visited after becoming Chancellor of Germany, in the spring of 1933, Hitler observed and was fascinated by Guderian's panzer unit. The soldiers taking part in the maneuvers may not have been terribly impressed: Guderian's earliest training vehicles had canvas sides through which an infantryman could stick his fist—this was the source of the rumor that later fooled the Polish troops—and even the succeeding tanks were made of thin sheet metal. But Hitler himself, who had a genuine eye for technical innovation, immediately saw the possibilities of the new tactics. "That's what I need!" he kept exclaiming. "That's what I want to have!" And in the next six years he backed up Guderian in his demand for armored divisions, against the generals who insisted that tanks could be used only in small packets to support the infantry.

As a mode of fighting, the concept of blitzkrieg had nonmilitary benefits that suited the Führer's warlike ambitions: "lightning war" would make for short, decisive campaigns that would place fewer burdens on the German economy and population; politically, such quick results would justify Hitler's aggressive foreign policy to his people, and help identify them ever more closely with him and the Nazi Party.

Turning the concept into reality was difficult, not only because of the opposition of conservative military men, but also because the six years from the Führer's assumption of power in 1933 to his own war deadline of 1939 was too short a time for the Reich's armaments plants to outfit Hitler's forces on the scale that he envisioned. His generals, and especially his admirals—whose shipbuilding plans were not scheduled to bear fruit until 1945—wanted him to wait for another four or five years. By this time, Germany's strength, in comparison with an enemy that had not yet begun to arm itself, would have been overwhelming.

But, as Hitler told visitors repeatedly in the spring of 1939, he was 50 years old, and if war had to come it had best be soon; in five years he might be too old to assume the conqueror's mantle of Napoleon. So he had elected to take a gamble of the kind that had paid off repeatedly in the past: to attack Poland with a force that was far from full strength.

Indeed, the Wehrmacht's weaknesses were considerable, and they had to be carefully concealed. Nazi propaganda released after the Polish campaign, especially in action films that were shown all over the world, was to create the impression that the entire German Army was a sophisticated mass of swift, heavily armed and armored vehicles—for that was what Hitler would have the world believe. And that is certainly what the rapid advance of the Germans into Poland seemed to prove.

The reality was far different: of the 44 divisions the Germans loosed on Poland, only six were real panzer divisions by Guderian's standards. The bulk of the fighting in Poland was done by old-style infantry divisions that had to tramp the dusty miles from battlefield to battlefield followed by their horse-drawn artillery and supply trains. Nor were the armored formations themselves as powerful as they were intended to be. The German factories had barely begun to turn out medium tanks, and most of the tanks that fought in Poland were thin-skinned, lightweight models armed with nothing more than machine guns.

Thus Hitler's gamble was a very considerable one. Furthermore, to concentrate against Poland such armor as he did have, along with the necessary air, artillery and infantry support, he had to take the even greater risk of throwing almost all of Germany's ground and air forces against the Poles. The pact with Russia had guaranteed that there would be no Soviet intervention against Germany; but Poland's allies in the west had promised that they would come to her support in case of attack. If most of the German Army and Air Force were concentrated in the east, only limited forces would remain to man the Siegfried line—the complex of fortifications hurriedly constructed over the last couple of years along the German-French border. Suppose the French, reacting to a threat to Poland, were to strike Germany in force? Hitler's generals were convinced that they might do so, and might in that case break through the lightly manned defenses of the Siegfried line into Germany.

But Hitler's intuition told him that the French would not attack on the ground—and Luftwaffe chief Hermann Göring was sure that his air force was more than equal to the challenge of defending Germany against assault from the sky. "The Ruhr will not be subjected to a single bomb!" Göring announced. "If an enemy bomb reaches the Ruhr, my name is not Hermann Göring!"

Encouraged in this manner, the German general staff had drawn up plans for an invasion of Poland that, although meticulously detailed, were basically quite simple. Poland formed a rounded salient projecting westward *(map, page 22)*, in effect, a plump victim poised between the two steely

arms of a massive German pincer; one arm threatened from Pomerania and East Prussia in the north, the other from Silesia and occupied Slovakia in the south. The plan called for these German arms to snap together in a single bloody crunch across Poland's waist.

At the western end of the salient, a comparatively light force of garrison troops barred any Polish adventure down the main Warsaw-Berlin road. Under General Fedor von Bock, 630,000 men were positioned to strike from the north, while 886,000 men were to drive from the south under General Gerd von Runstedt, in the general direction of Warsaw. The combined force was to be supported by almost 2,000 warplanes and 1,700 tanks. When the pincers met, the bulk of the Polish Army would be encircled and destroyed.

To stand up to this force, Poland had an army of 1.75 million men including its largely unmobilized reserves, with 935 aircraft and 500 tanks, many of them obsolete. It was a fine army by the standards of 1920, when it had last fought —against an invading Soviet thrust commanded by General Mikhail N. Tukhachevsky. The Poles had stopped the Soviets at the gates of Warsaw and chased them back into Russia. But by the standards of 1939 the Polish force was hopelessly inadequate and unprepared. Partly from a shortage of money, partly from lack of manpower trained in mechanized warfare, and partly from sheer overconfidence, the Poles had failed to modernize more than a small fraction of their forces; the few late-model Polish aircraft, tanks and antiaircraft and antitank artillery were not ineffective by comparison with similar German equipment—they were only critically inferior in numbers.

The Polish Army found itself called upon to defend a long, meandering frontier that, for the most part, was just an arbitrary line drawn over the north-European plain. Except for the Carpathians in the south, Poland had nothing in the way of rivers or mountains as natural frontiers. The original Polish-German border, as drawn in 1919, had been a vulnerable 1,250 miles in length. After the Germans absorbed Czechoslovakia between 1938 and 1939, the Poles' border with German-dominated territory became extended to a new total of 1,750 miles. The Poles had strung barbed wire, dug trenches and set gun emplacements at key points to form a thin defense system along this frontier.

General Heinz Guderian, the principal architect of Germany's devastating blitzkrieg strategy, uses a periscope to observe his tanks. Guderian realized the potential of an armored striking force as a young officer during World War I when infantry was routinely slaughtered in attacking entrenched defenses—but primitive tanks were able to break through.

To man these defenses adequately would have stretched their army, even if it had been fully mobilized. But the forces available on September 1 fell far short of full strength; the effective number was about one million men. Under pressure from their French and British allies, the Poles had delayed ordering general mobilization. Paris and London had feared the move might provoke Hitler. Thus, tens of thousands of Polish reservists were still waiting in railway stations or were riding in freight cars toward their units on the morning of the attack.

Besides being undermobilized, the Poles could not provide their forces with weapons and other supplies for a long war because they lacked a strong industrial base. In any protracted war, the Polish Army would have had to be supplied from abroad. Spare parts for its vehicles, for instance, would have had to be shipped from factories in France to Marseille, there to be loaded on cargo vessels for the 2,000-mile passage across the Mediterranean and up the Aegean, through the Dardanelles, the Bosporus and the Black Sea. Unloaded at a Rumanian port, the material would then have been transferred to that country's single-track railroad and hauled 500 miles to the Polish border, thence to be transshipped to the front via a Polish transportation system inadequate even for peacetime needs.

An additional handicap for Poland's defense was the polyglot nature of the population; the army could not count on the undivided loyalty of its recruits or on that of many civilians in the battle zones. At least 30 per cent of those living in the Polish Republic were not ethnic Poles. There were half a dozen sizable minorities—including two million Germans—and all had grievances. The Lithuanians in the northeast claimed that the Polish provincial capital of Vilna should be the Lithuanian national capital of Vilnius. The Ukrainian and Belorussian peasants of the eastern provinces were among the poorest and most downtrodden in Europe; in the last days of the campaign, Polish armies retreating through these regions marched at night by the sinister illumination of flames from manor houses and from Catholic churches set afire by Russian Orthodox peasants to pay off centuries of old scores against their Polish landlords. The Jews, though they had every reason to hate and fear Hitler, felt scant loyalty to a Polish government that treated them like second-class citizens. The Germans in the western provinces had a clear memory of their preeminence in those regions before 1918; they could hardly wait for the arrival of the Nazi armies so that they could rejoin the Fatherland —and lord it once again over their Polish neighbors.

Beset by all these weaknesses, the Polish military planners found themselves faced by a strategic nightmare. They had only two possible choices, and neither held much hope. The Poles could elect to stand all along the frontier, in which case they would be taking the full brunt of an attack by a superior enemy on an inadequately fortified defense line. Or they could adopt a more cautious strategy and concentrate their main forces on a natural line such as that formed by the San, Vistula and Narew rivers. But this would mean abandoning the western provinces that were the richest part of their country, including its coal mines and most of its industry. And it went against the Polish grain to give up any territory whatever: The country had been resurrected only 21 years before after more than 150 years of foreign rule, and every inch of its newly independent soil was sacred. So the Polish generals settled on a plan that was a compromise between the two main options: fight initially on the frontiers, then fall back to prepared positions, while waging a mobile campaign that would employ sharp counterattacks against enemy flanks and spearheads. The goal was to hold the invaders back long enough for the British and French to come to Poland's aid by attacking Germany from the west—although some officers were still talking about a "march to Berlin" on the night of August 31.

But there was no march to Berlin, and no help came. The German armor penetrated and shattered the Polish front in the first two or three days of battle; thereafter, the Poles had no chance to form another front. The only thing that held up the advance in many places was the caution of some of the senior German generals, who insisted that the tanks wait for the infantry to catch up with them.

Indeed, the tanks could not do everything. Panzer forces were at a disadvantage in swampy forests where tanks bogged down while attacking remnants of the Polish forces that used the woods to hide and regroup, and that sometimes sallied out to make punishing assaults on isolated German detachments. Panzer divisions were held up—at least temporarily—by large inhabited areas; General Walther von

Reichenau's tanks raced, in less than a week, from the south to the suburbs of Warsaw, a distance of 150 miles. But barricades of trolley cars stopped them in the streets and their infantry had to fight from house to house. Guderian, who had been transferred to the northeastern end of the line, plunged deep through the Polish rear to Brest-Litovsk, but his attempt to take the town's massive old citadel by storm was momentarily foiled by a single obsolete Renault tank that the Poles had jammed into the gateway.

For the Poles, such resourcefulness and courage were not enough. In the general confusion that soon became the defenders' worst enemy, General Anders' experience was typical. On the third day of the war he was transferred from his divisional command in the north to another unit at Mlava. He spent two whole days covering a few miles to reach his new post, pushing through and around burning villages and roads solid for miles with stalled traffic. He was strafed by German planes and suffered wounds in his back that were to keep him in crippling pain for weeks. When he finally joined the two infantry divisions he was to command, he found them in disorderly flight.

Anders moved the units to Plock, on the Vistula, only to receive orders to blow up the bridge he had intended to cross, and proceed, instead, to Modlin. Scarcely had he reached the Modlin area when he was ordered to yet another command in a forest on the outskirts of Warsaw. He traveled two more days and nights with bone-weary men and thirst-maddened horses through the milling chaos of fugitives. Southwest of Warsaw, Anders managed to mount a surprise attack on a German force, taking many prisoners. But owing to the breakdown of communications and a deepening failure of the Polish command system, the units that should have fought alongside Anders never got their orders, and the operation ended in heavy losses and defeat.

When Anders, in a vain search for reliable information, entered Warsaw on September 11, he found a capital partly destroyed by bombing, crammed with refugees, and running short of supplies. The population was burning with patriotic fervor, anxious to fight the Germans to the last breath but totally confused as to how to go about it. The government had left on September 4, and the High Command had followed on the 7th, beginning an odyssey that would take the top military and civilian leaders in a couple of weeks into neighboring Rumania, which was still on friendly terms with Poland, though a future German ally.

They left behind orders to fight to the bitter end—an end which could not be put off for more than a few days. Loudspeakers blared out martial music and contradictory commands: now they were ordering all men capable of bearing arms to remain in Warsaw, now they were ordering everyone to leave. As the German bombs and shells fell and fires spread out of control, the wild rumors typical of wartime circulated: the French were pouring over the Rhine on their way to Berlin; General Tadeusz Kutrzeba had routed the Germans west of Warsaw.

The French were nowhere near ready to attack. General Kutrzeba, however, was. He was commander of the biggest and best of the Polish armies, which a foolhardy battle plan had placed around Poznan in the extreme west of the country. He had been forced to retire eastward to evade the lightning German advances which threatened to cut him off from Warsaw. Then he saw the chance to hit back.

General von Rundstedt, commanding the German southern wing, had advanced so fast that he was running out of troops to guard his left flank. He had asked for more cavalry to keep track of the Poles in this wooded area. However, the German army was short of mounted troops. So when General Kutrzeba came charging southward across the Bzu-

ANGLIO! TWOJE DZIEŁO!

"Britain! This is your work!" shouts an anguished Polish soldier to Neville Chamberlain, shown disdainfully turning his back on slaughtered civilians in this Polish-language poster produced by Nazi propagandists. Designed to dissuade Polish soldiers from fleeing to Britain, where they could fight again, the poster contained a measure of bitter truth. Though Britain declared war on Germany just after Hitler struck Poland, no British fighting men appeared on the Continent until well after the Polish surrender.

ra River on September 10, he achieved a tactical surprise and badly mauled the single German division that was strung along its eastern bank. There was a momentary panic at German headquarters, and if the other Polish armies had been able to act in concert they might have made things difficult for the invaders. But they were isolated and out of touch, while the Germans, with their command of the air and their superior mobility, could rapidly bring up reinforcements to seal off any Polish breakthrough. Within two days, Kutrzeba's army was pinched off by converging German attacks. A handful of his troops made it to Warsaw; the remainder surrendered on September 17.

With their armies everywhere in flight or surrounded, with all their big cities captured or under siege, with supplies of everything running short and no glimmer of help from their allies, the Poles were now in a critical situation. Their only chance to keep up the struggle at all was to extricate as many troops as they could and hole up in the southeastern corner of the country, where there remained the friendly border with Rumania and a chance to communicate through that country with the outside world. With luck, they might elude their pursuers; as the German units approached these southeastern provinces of Poland, their supply lines were being stretched dangerously long, their troops needed rest, and their transport was beginning to wear out from the Polish roads. Besides, the rains might come any day.

The Poles' last thin hope for reprieve was shattered on the 17th when, with no more declaration of war than Hitler had made, Stalin picked up the chips he had won through his pact with the Führer and sent an immense concentration of troops across the undefended eastern frontier of Poland. Stalin had timed the move shrewdly. Letting the Germans do all the fighting, he had only to collect the spoils; at no time—especially not now—would the Poles have been capable of fighting a two-front war against enemies who were among the greatest military powers on earth.

Within a few days a shocked world was seeing photographs of officers of the German and Russian armies, the most irreconcilable of enemies before the signing of the Nazi-Soviet agreement, cordially shaking hands at the border of their respective occupation zones. For all practical purposes, Poland was finished; the war was over.

But the Poles kept on fighting. Warsaw, its civilian pop-

ulation swollen with refugees, threatened with famine and disease, under continuous pounding by German planes and guns, struggled grimly on. When crowds of refugees tried to flee the battered city, the Germans drove them back so that the Poles could be more easily starved into surrender. And the threat of starvation was a major factor in forcing the Warsaw garrison to capitulate at last on September 27; the fortress of Modlin held out a day longer. Other pockets of resistance went on fighting and it was only on the 6th of October that the last organized Polish fighting force gave up —at Kock, a town southeast of Warsaw. Here a diehard garrison of 17,000 men had clung tenaciously to their encircled stronghold, until it finally became obvious that no help could reach them—or would ever be sent.

A few bits and pieces were saved from the wreckage. Some destroyers and submarines of Poland's tiny navy, ducking past superior German forces in the Baltic, got away in the fog, sailed around Denmark into the North Sea and eventually reached England, where they were to fight bravely alongside the Royal Navy for the rest of the War.

Some 100,000 Polish soldiers, a fraction of the force that

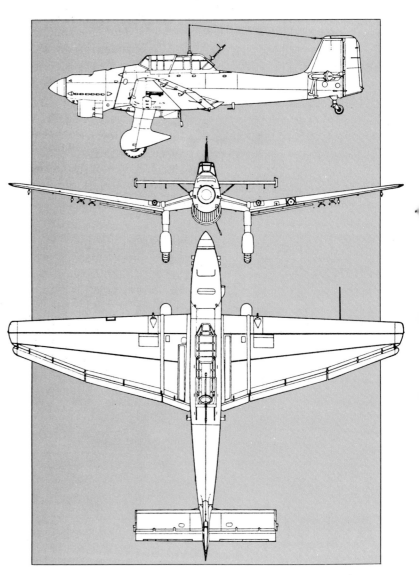

Perhaps the most terrifying and innovative weapon in Hitler's arsenal for lightning war was the Ju-87 Stuka dive bomber. Deadly accurate, with a 2,000-pound maximum bomb load that it could deliver just before pulling out of a vertical plunge, the Stuka was dubbed the "shrieking vulture" by its prey, who compared its spat-covered, fixed undercarriage (top) to the talons of an evil bird. Other distinctive features of the Ju-87 were its inverted gull wing (center) and its squared-off tail (bottom). Excellent as a supporting weapon in the ground warfare of Poland and France —particularly against bridges, troop columns and enemy tanks—the Stuka proved to be helpless in aerial combat with fast British fighters.

started out, made it to Rumania in the wake of their leaders and later formed Free Polish units that fought with the French and British. Many more had their flight cut off by the Russian invasion and suffered the horrors of Stalin's prison camps—starvation, floggings, massacre. When Russia was attacked in its turn a couple of years later, the Polish survivors, under General Anders, were allowed to leave and fight the Germans again in North Africa and Italy.

The German and Russian aggressors had not waited for the end of Polish resistance to carve up their victim. The original pact signed by foreign ministers Vyacheslav Molotov and Joachim von Ribbentrop in August had been ambiguous about the eventual fate of Poland; Russia and Germany may have been thinking at the time of setting up a Polish rump state in the center of the country after they had annexed the peripheral provinces. The August pact provided for a partition line between spheres of influence running approximately through the center of Poland. Stalin now proposed to leave central Poland to the Germans, retaining only the eastern regions where a majority of the population was of Ukrainian or Belorussian stock. In return, he demanded a free hand in Lithuania—although the pact had originally allocated that Baltic area to Germany—and possession of all the oil fields in southeast Poland, from which he promised to send 30,000 tons of crude oil yearly to Germany.

Hitler was not happy about this change in plans, but he agreed, and the new partition line along the Bug, San and Narew rivers was duly ratified. The eastern provinces were incorporated into the Soviet Union. The western provinces, inhabited by many ethnic Germans, were annexed by the Reich. For the ethnically Polish population of the central portions, Hitler was about to provide an object lesson in how Germany would treat conquered territory. Whatever he did not actually annex was established as a Nazi fief called the Government General, and its function was stated very succinctly by Hans Frank, the party official who was to be its ruler for the next four and a half years: "The Poles will be the slaves of the Greater German World Reich." The means to achieve this end was to be naked brutality and terror.

Hitler had warned his generals before the campaign started that there would be no room for humanitarian scruples in Poland. Some, at least, of the generals were slow to catch on to what he meant. On September 19, an SS private and a military policeman, who were overseeing a work detail of 50 Polish Jews, became dissatisfied with their charges' performance. They herded the Jews into a synagogue and killed them all. The military authorities, still under the illusion that they were fighting a traditional war, were horrified and had the two killers court-martialed. The prosecutor demanded the death penalty. After deliberation, the court found the two men guilty of manslaughter and condemned them to three and nine years imprisonment respectively. General Georg von Küchler, under whom both men were serving, found these sentences outrageously light and insisted on an appeal to a higher court in Berlin. This court upheld the three-year sentence for the SS man, finding extenuation on the grounds that "he was particularly sensitive to the sight of Jews," and had acted "quite unpremeditatedly in a spirit of youthful enthusiasm." Both men soon were granted amnesty and never served a day in prison.

Officers of the German Army who disapproved of such leniency quickly learned that it was wiser to look the other way and to keep their misgivings to themselves. During the subsequent years of the War, General von Küchler himself was noted for his subservience to Hitler's slightest wish.

The shape of the future was spelled out at a meeting between top Army and Nazi figures on September 19, which was curtly noted by General Halder in his diary. Nazi policy in Poland was summed up by the word "housecleaning," a euphemism for physical extermination. The Jews were to be "housecleaned"; so were the Polish intellectuals, clergy, nobility—any group that might provide leaders for a potential resistance. The generals insisted that they wanted no part of this; as Halder recorded their feelings in his diary, "housecleaning must be deferred until Army has withdrawn and country turned over to civil administration," which was to be by early December. The Army could then direct its full attention to its lofty task of planning new military campaigns while the SS and the Gestapo drenched Poland in blood.

Thus Hitler had every reason to be content with the way things were going. He had annihilated a stubborn enemy, at minimal cost. He had a quiescent if not friendly frontier on his eastern flank. Now he could turn all his powers as a strategist, his thoroughly vindicated intuition, and the full-armed might of Germany against his enemies in the West.

FIRST FLASH OF LIGHTNING WAR

On September 1, 1939, the first day of the invasion of Poland, German infantrymen symbolically break a wooden barricade on the Polish border.

A PANZER SWEEP THROUGH POLAND

Stuka dive bombers skim the trees ahead of a German armored car in an attack on Polish troop concentrations and supply depots down the road.

To members of the German force massed along the Polish border on the morning of September 1, 1939, their own power seemed awesome. As thousands of tanks, armored cars and troop-carrying vehicles started their engines, the din was echoed from a sky filled with Luftwaffe planes. One young infantryman, looking on through the first minutes of the Polish invasion, excitedly scrawled in his diary: "It is a wonderful feeling, now, to be a German. . . . The row of tanks has no end. A quarter of an hour, tanks, tanks, tanks."

In the ensuing days, these tanks, planes and other engines of modern war knifed through the astonished—and outmoded—Polish Army with a speed that put a new word into the lexicon of battle: blitzkrieg. But behind this terrifying spearhead of armor, it was infantrymen like the young diarist who consolidated the armor's gains, and did the dirtiest of the war's work. Each man carried a load of equipment that, though designed to be as light as possible for combat efficiency, was nonetheless formidable: a Mauser rifle, two grenades, 60 rounds of ammunition, as well as gas mask, canteen, trenching tool, mess kit and rucksack.

In the first two weeks of the blitzkrieg the front rank of foot soldiers made forced marches of as much as 40 miles a day, trying to catch up with the dust-churning tanks. The young diarist complained of "terrible thirst" in the September heat, of sore feet and of being unable to wash. But he took heart as he saw everywhere the evidence of the army's might: "vehicles shot to pieces . . . soldiers and horses laid out flat by our bombers." And when his unit was rescued from a bloody firefight by dive-bombing Stukas, he wrote that "we love our Luftwaffe and are proud of it."

Meanwhile, far ahead in the van, motorized units sped through villages and across country, bypassing or outflanking Polish positions. Some of these columns traveled 125 miles in little more than a week—a thrust that brought them to the outskirts of Warsaw. There, weary but elated, they waited for the infantry and sized up the Polish capital in preparation for a final battle that they thought would last only a few more days.

During an infantry assault, a German soldier, supported by two of his comrades, cocks his arm to throw a "potato masher" hand grenade.

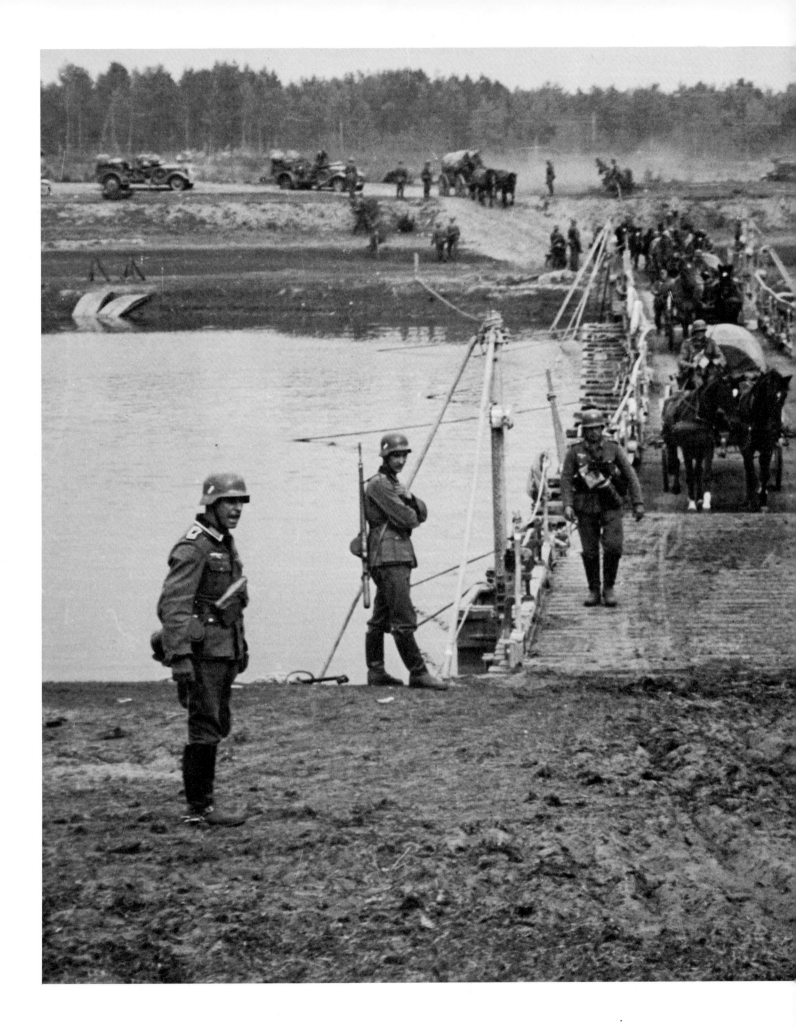

Impatient at the pace of supply wagons filing across a river in Poland, a Wehrmacht sergeant (left) tongue-lashes a driver for moving his team too slowly.

A farm wagon hugs the shoulder to give more road room to advancing German vehicles.

Confident that Polish snipers have been eliminated, crewmen ride outside their turrets.

German reconnaissance motorcycles roll past Polish farmers in a village of thatch-roofed houses.

Slowed by tough Polish defenders at the outskirts of Warsaw, German soldiers in a trench provide cover for comrades advancing past derelict trolley cars.

DEFIANT STAND IN A DOOMED CITY

By September 14, Wehrmacht armor and infantry had surrounded Warsaw, and the Germans, under a flag of truce, delivered a demand to the Poles for unconditional surrender. But instead of giving up, the people of Warsaw began to fortify the city.

Men, women and children worked into the night digging trenches in parks, playgrounds and vacant lots. Wealthy Warsaw aristocrats were chauffeured to defense sites, where they toiled alongside office workers. Trolley cars were thrown across thoroughfares; barricades of cars and furniture were erected in narrow streets.

When the German tanks jumped off for the attack, instead of blitzing through as they had on the Polish plains, they were stopped dead—in many cases by civilians who dashed boldly into the streets to toss burning rags under the vehicles, causing them to catch fire and explode. German infantrymen who had mopped up the Polish Army in open country were pinned down by snipers, who seemed to have turned every house into a pillbox. Warsaw Radio helped carry on the battle in its own way. Every 30 seconds it transmitted portions of a polonaise by Polish composer Frédéric Chopin to tell the world that the capital was still in Polish hands.

Angered by the unexpected setback, the German High Command decided to pound the stubborn citadel into submission. In round-the-clock raids, bombers knocked out flourmills, gasworks, power plants and reservoirs, then sowed the residential areas with incendiaries. One witness, passing scenes of carnage, enumerated the horrors: "Everywhere corpses, wounded humans, killed horses." And everywhere —in public squares, gardens and even footpaths—hastily dug graves of the thousands killed in the attack.

Finally food ran out, and famished Poles, as one man described it, "cut off pieces of flesh as soon as a horse fell, leaving only the skeleton." On September 28, 1939, Warsaw Radio replaced the polonaise with a funeral dirge. The capital had fallen. But the city's agony did not end with defeat. Within hours of the surrender, SS squads began rounding up Jews and other designated enemies of the Reich. Some were summarily shot; others, perhaps less fortunate, were shipped out to prison camps in the first major phase of Hitler's "Extraordinary Pacification Action"—the Nazi euphemism for mass murder.

Warsaw residents dig trenches for the city's small stock of antiaircraft guns. By the time the Germans began to break into the city it was crisscrossed by 13 miles

Smoke rises from the Warsaw gasworks during one of the Luftwaffe attacks that reduced vital urban services to mounds of smoldering rubble.

of trenches that served as gun emplacements, and as shelters and tank traps.

Hungry Poles in Warsaw's finest residential district carve up a horse that was killed by German bombs; one pedestrian looks on casually and others ignore a scene that had become common in the besieged and starving city. Most Poles had no meat of any kind; and some could find nothing whatever to eat through the ultimate days of the battle.

Poles race for cover moments after German fire bombs hit houses in a working-class neighborhood. Luftwaffe pilots, engaging in virtually nonstop raids, destroyed one fourth of the city of Warsaw in just four days.

Bombed-out survivors wander down a littered street among the shells of Warsaw buildings. "There were fires every day," recalled one citizen, who added that "we slept fully dressed, with our suitcases containing the most indispensable objects next to our beds."

A Warsaw woman hurries past coffins in the rubble of a road. The seige killed 12,000 civilians; many were entombed in collapsed buildings.

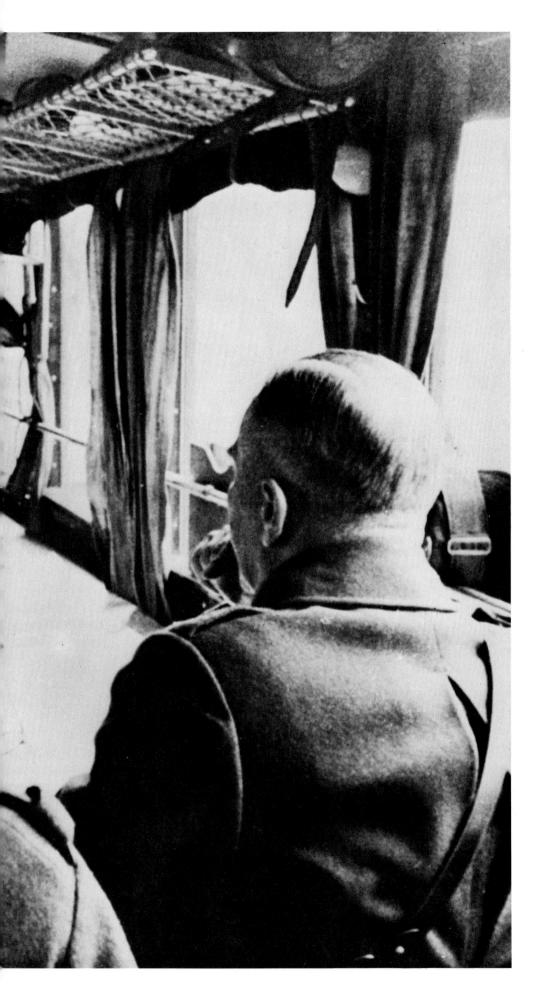

In a railway car in Rakow just outside Warsaw, Polish officers (foreground) formally surrender Warsaw to German General Johannes Blaskowitz, seated between two aides at left. The defenders capitulated only when they had run out of medical supplies, food and water.

A day after the surrender, Polish Jews wait
nervously in a railroad station after
being rounded up by Hitler's SS, the elite
Nazi security corps. The SS was under orders to
segregate and deport or shoot Jews and
any other Poles judged to be intellectually
dissident or otherwise undesirable.

SS officers frisk a Warsaw citizen. Anyone
caught carrying anything that could be construed
as a weapon or hiding any sort of arms
at his home was executed without a trial
—sometimes right on the spot.

SS men jump from a staff car to grab a suspect. Sudden arrests by such flying squads became a common—and dreaded—occurrence following the capitulation of Poland.

In a Jewish community center, prisoners await grilling by German security officers. Within a year after the fall of Poland, 1.5 million Poles, including 300,000 Jews, were expelled from their dwellings and their jobs and sent to towns in the central part of the country. Their homes in western Poland, which had been annexed to the Reich, were taken over by Germans.

Before a sparse audience of curious Poles, German infantrymen led by mounted officers march in a victory parade through Warsaw's Pilsudski Square.

2

It was a gay evening at the German Officers Club in the Westphalian air base at Münster on January 9, 1940. Over convivial rounds of beer, two Luftwaffe majors struck up an acquaintance and hatched a plan for their mutual benefit. Erich Hoenmanns was a retread, a World War I flyer who was eating his heart out at being kept in a chairborne post running the local airfield. Hellmuth Reinberger, on the other hand, was an ambitious Luftwaffe staff officer with hopes of rising high in the command structure. He was due at an important staff meeting in Cologne the next day, which would require an overnight journey on a jolting, overcrowded and unreliable train, and he had horrid visions of arriving late, unshaven and unpresentable.

Major Hoenmanns was delighted to be of service. If he could manage to clock enough hours flying light planes on courier missions and the like, he had reason to believe he could go back to active flight duty. Suppose that he were to fly Major Reinberger to Cologne at dawn? Reinberger would arrive at the great city on the Rhine as fresh as a daisy; Hoenmanns would get in his flying time, and also a chance to visit his wife, who lived nearby. No sooner proposed than enthusiastically agreed. Next morning the two officers were on their way in a new-model Messerschmitt Taifun scout plane, heading west from Münster toward the Rhine through a clear blue sky.

The air did not stay clear for long. Wisps of fog appeared, and built into thick cover. Little doubts, the precursors of panic, began to spring up in Major Hoenmanns' mind. The Taifun was a faster plane than he was used to flying—especially when it was pushed by the strong easterly tail wind blowing that day. Where the devil was the Rhine? The ground was covered with frost, the streams were frozen, and whenever there was a fleeting break in the fog, all he could see below was solid white.

As the minutes ticked by, the panic grew. Suppose he had overshot the Rhine? He had no maps of the country west of the river. He had never thought of asking Major Reinberger if he had any maps. And Major Reinberger had never thought of telling him that his briefcase contained maps, all right—and much, much more. Reinberger was carrying a copy of sections of the secret operational plan for the German invasion of Holland and Belgium, which was due to start in exactly one week—documents that he and all other

A SEASON OF BLUNDERS

officers had been specifically ordered never under any circumstances to take up in an airplane.

Hoenmanns was circling wildly by now, hoping to catch a glimpse of some familiar piece of scenery. Finally he spotted a river. Perhaps it was the Rhine. He circled lower, and was peering anxiously around him—when his engine ran out of fuel and stopped running. There was a field ahead of him surrounded by hedges. Amply justifying the Luftwaffe's lack of faith in his flying abilities, he came down where the field was narrowest, sheered off both wings on trees and ended up nose down against a hedge. Amazingly, neither of the flyers was badly hurt. As they pulled themselves out of the wreck, some peasants came up to see what had happened. They spoke no German. Hoenmanns' worst fears were realized. The river he had sighted was not the Rhine but the Meuse. They were down in Belgium.

Reinberger had the presence of mind to duck behind a hedge and set fire to his precious papers. But he was too late; he had barely set a match to the files when Belgian border guards came up to investigate, and put out the flames before they could do much more than scorch some of the documents. In any case, the two German officers clearly had no business where they were. They were taken to the nearby town of Mechelen-sur-Meuse for questioning.

It quickly became clear to the Belgian officials there that they had stumbled on to something extraordinary. At first they believed the two majors might be on a spy mission. Then, when they examined the papers, they thought that the plans might be a plant, a false alarm to induce both the Belgians and the Western Allies to rush to arms and give away their own plans for troop movements at the outbreak of hostilities. However, the Belgian officers soon convinced themselves that the papers were genuine. It would have been impossible to fake the plane crash. In corroboration, Major Reinberger's eagerness to destroy the papers appeared pathetically genuine. When he failed in a second attempt to burn them by shoving them into a stove during his interrogation, he tore his hair, banged his head against a wall, and sobbed that his career was ruined, that he had betrayed the Fatherland.

When the news reached Berlin a few hours later, Hitler did some wall-banging himself. "The Führer was possessed," General Wilhelm Keitel reported later, "foaming at the mouth, pounding the wall with his fist and hurling the lowest insults at the 'incompetents and traitors of the General Staff,' whom he threatened with the death penalty. Even Göring came in for a terrible scene." In turn, Göring vented his own wrath by summarily firing General Hellmuth Felmy, Reinberger's commanding officer, while the angry Führer put through rigorous orders for the further strengthening of already stringent measures protecting the security of high-level military procedures and decisions.

While Berlin was busy closing its barn doors, the high commands in Brussels, Paris and London went into little cyclones of basically directionless activity. For one of the oddest aspects of this strangely dunderheaded misadventure is that almost nobody—on the German or on the Allied side—quite knew what to do about it. The accident confirmed an imminent and perhaps mortal threat to the Low Countries, France and Britain. But it also offered them, in a neatly wrapped gift package, what appeared to be a golden opportunity to chuck their own, uninspired defensive strategy against the Germans in the west, and perhaps beat their opponents to the punch.

On the other hand, the plane crash and loss of their secret papers confronted Hitler and his staff with an urgent need to switch their own plans, unless, of course, the Allies might be doubly fooled by the Germans' standing pat. As subsequent events unfolded, the incident and its aftermath became the perfect symbol of the mood on both sides of the line during the eight-month pause in fighting after the Polish defeat, when indecision, ineptitude and lassitude enveloped nearly everyone involved in making decisions—with the exception of Adolf Hitler and his bolder generals.

The first question that Berlin asked itself was the obvious one: had the papers really been destroyed, as Major Reinberger assured the German military attaché they had been when he was allowed to make contact with the German embassy in Brussels? If they had not been destroyed, should the Germans go ahead with their attack plans anyway, or should they change them?

To change would be relatively simple. For almost four months Hitler and his top generals had been wrangling about how to defeat the Allies, and as a result the number of plan changes and postponements that already had been discussed was considerable.

In fact Hitler had set the precedent for continual reexamination and change back on September 27, while the Polish campaign was still in progress. He intended, he told his generals, to turn immediately and take the offensive against the West. The generals were horrified. They were counting on a positional war on the western frontiers, at least for several months when more troops would have been mobilized and brought up to a proper state of training, and when there was some hope of good weather in the spring. But Hitler had been adamant: an offensive must be launched before winter set in; it must be underway before the Allies had time to marshal their forces to occupy the Low Countries.

Actually, at this stage, Hitler's goals were limited; he simply wanted to occupy the Low Countries and the Channel coastline from Ostend west to Calais. Nevertheless, the Army's Commander-in-Chief, General Walther von Brauchitsch, and his Chief of Staff, Franz Halder, presented a report arguing strongly against an autumn offensive. The Führer brushed it aside. Two weeks later he issued his Directive No. 6 for the Conduct of the War, calling for an attack through Belgium, Luxembourg and Holland "with as much strength and at as early a date as possible." He told his personal staff he wanted to start by November 12.

Brauchitsch and Halder were so appalled by what they both regarded as Hitler's military madness that they held a long conference on October 14, during which, in guarded terms, they envisaged the possibility of "fundamental changes," that is, getting rid of Hitler. The scheme was to use part of the Army to remove and "liquidate" Hitler, if he could not be talked out of his offensive. The signal that would trigger this conspiracy was to be the receipt of the formal order to the General Staff for the attack jump-off. Brauchitsch utterly failed to dissuade the Führer from his aggressive purpose; Hitler raged and browbeat the commander-in-chief to the edge of a nervous breakdown.

Although backed by numerous co-conspirators, neither Halder nor other like-minded generals had the ultimate courage to assume responsibility for giving the orders that would be necessary in order to unleash the Army against their leader. "Halder," grumbled one conspirator in his diary, "is not equal to the situation either in caliber or in authority." In any event, like many of the other schemes, plots and conspiracies concocted by the generals against Hitler,

nothing ever came of this. The bulk of the Army command preferred, instead, to sabotage the leader's plans by giving the appearance of going along with his proposal while dragging their feet at every opportunity.

On October 19 the generals dutifully produced their first overall plan for an offensive. Widely criticized for being singularly unimaginative, it provided only for a straight thrust westward through Holland and northern Belgium to the Channel ports. But this was all that Hitler had asked for; though he was dissatisfied with the plan, he had to accept it because he had nothing better at hand. At a meeting on October 25, the Führer asked Brauchitsch—with remarkable prescience, as it turned out—if it might not be possible to put the main weight of the attack in southern Belgium instead, pushing it through the forested region of the Ardennes toward Sedan. The generals told him that it would not be possible; they considered that hilly, wooded area to be unsuitable for massed armor—as did the French. But the idea remained in the back of Hitler's mind.

November came, and so did bad weather, the beginning of the severest European winter in decades. What the generals could not accomplish the meteorologists did: Hitler hesitated. The offensive was postponed to the 19th, then to the 22nd, the 26th, December 9, December 11, December 17, January 1, January 9. Finally, on the assurance of one of Göring's weather experts that two weeks of "clear winter weather" could be expected, the assault was set for January 17. All this while, considerable tinkering had been going on with the original plan but it still called for the main thrust of the attack to be in the north, around Liège, for a smash through to the Channel coast.

Then, in mid-January of 1940, just as the scenario seemed ready to open, came the mishap of the two flying majors, and along with it the alarming probability that at least part of the plan had fallen into Western hands. "If the enemy is in possession of all the files," General Alfred Jodl noted in his diary, "the situation is catastrophic."

In the West, meanwhile, Belgian, French and British generals and statesmen sat in perplexed concentration, worrying and debating about the bizarre episode of the strayed Taifun. The Belgians, who continued to believe the documents were genuine, put their troops on alert. The French,

EASY LIFE IN A SUPERTRENCH

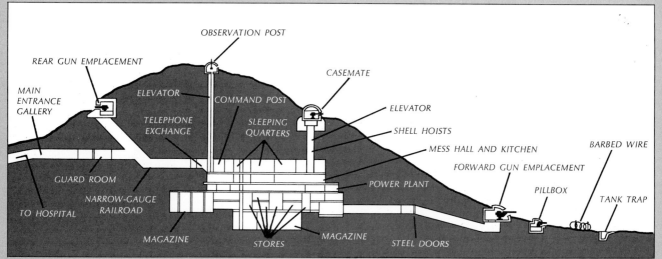

This cutaway profile of a Maginot fort shows its main elements: multilevel areas connected by tunnels to gun and observation posts.

After almost losing to the Germans in World War I, the French were determined to make their land impregnable. Beginning in 1930, at a cost of over $200 million and seven years' labor, they built an 87-mile-long string of underground forts facing Germany.

Named after André Maginot, the Defense Minister when work began, the Line was a masterpiece of static defense. At its forward edge were tank traps; behind lay barbed wire and pillboxes. Next came rows of gun emplacements walled in concrete 10 feet thick and armed with machine guns and antitank weapons ranging from 37mm to 135mm. Located at three- to five-mile intervals were immense fortresses (above), buried as deep as 100 feet underground.

Within these forts, up to 1,200 men lived for three-month tours. They had sun lamps and went topside to plant roses; still, their most deadly enemy was boredom. "We're not fighting the Germans," one man said, "we're fighting l'ennui."

But when the Wehrmacht began its attack in earnest, the real enemy was the concept of the supertrench itself. The age of static warfare was over and even the strongest fortress would soon prove no match for the maneuverability of German panzers.

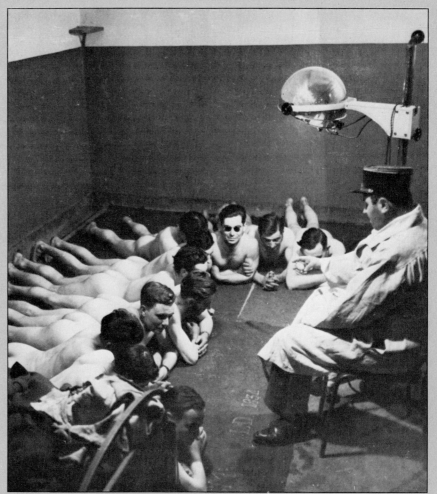

Soldiers deep underground take time off from their duties to bask in the rays of a sun lamp.

who were not sure, nonetheless rushed forces to the Belgian frontier—where they were halted in freezing rain and snow, waiting to be invited into Belgium. They never were, because the Brussels government, mistrustful of Paris to the last, refused to permit French troops on Belgian soil until the German Army had actually violated the frontier—even though Belgium had previously agreed to accept Allied aid in the event of an attack. The French, for their part, mistrusted the British. Ambiguous or misunderstood messages involving the captured German plans passed between Brussels, London and Paris; these garbled communications left each of the three parties sure that the other two were lying —or in any event were holding back part of the truth. Unfortunately, in several regards, the suspicions were justified.

Fearful of giving Hitler an excuse to strike, the Belgians —and the Dutch—not only refused entry to French and British troops, but also refused to let the Allies make systematic analyses of Belgian and Dutch defenses. Belgium, moreover, also declined to give Allied intelligence officers any access to the documents captured from the German majors. Only a précis was shared. One result was that many French and British generals went on regarding the German plans in Belgian hands as a plant. And some of these commanders shrugged off the plans on grounds that nothing much could be done about them even if they were real.

Nor were the Allies as yet doing much of anything else to ward off the fearful and imminent danger that threatened them. Although their High Command gave an outward impression of extreme activity and bustle, shuffling papers from early morning until late at night, they actually were mired in a profound intellectual lethargy.

The fact was that Britain and France had come into the War in the first place without adequate armaments. Their official declarations of war had come on September 3, two days after Germany had attacked Poland—and six hours apart, the Allies not having synchronized even this momentous action. But backing up the declarations of war, they made no major military move to help the Poles. This was only one of a sequence of tragic Allied errors, born of both muddleheadedness and extreme caution.

Throughout the Wehrmacht's planning for the blitzkrieg in Poland, the German generals had been deeply worried that France would immediately retaliate by throwing its army across the Rhine. As a countermeasure, the Germans had constructed a deep zone of concrete fortifications and of antitank obstacles—the West Wall or Siegfried Line—along their western frontier. In the fall of 1939, however, the Siegfried Line was not yet complete, and its garrison was heavily outnumbered and even outgunned by the French, for the Germans had all their best troops and equipment hundreds of miles away in Poland. An all-out attack by the French on the West Wall would have been terribly costly, but it had a chance to succeed; and it would certainly have taken pressure off the Poles.

But a chance, and especially a costly chance, was one thing the French generals were not about to take. Most of them had commanded brigades and divisions in World War I, and had seen the best young men of their nation mowed down in attacks on fortified lines. Everything in their experience pointed to the superiority of a well-armed defense in modern warfare. They knew that neither their government nor their people would stand for a bloodbath on the 1914-1918 model, when 1.5 million men had died, out of a population of only 40 million.

Thus, prudence was the watchword dictating, for example, that before any offensive could begin, there had to be a pulverizing artillery bombardment with thousands of heavy guns. These were in critically short supply. Although France had developed some effective types of artillery since 1918, it had been unable to afford many of the new guns. And most of the World War I heavy guns had been disassembled years before, rustproofed with petroleum grease, and stored in depots. After the declaration of war, these guns had to be located, identified, degreased, reassembled, loaded onto flatcars or trucks, moved up to the frontier, emplaced, tested. By that time—near the end of the third week of September—Poland was as good as lost; there seemed to be no further point in talking about an attack.

Shortly after, the bulk of the German Army moved west from Poland and took up positions along the French frontier. The united German force was approximately as strong as the French Army; and that, under the prevailing military doctrine, made any frontal attack out of the question. So the French holed up in their fortresses on the Maginot Line and prepared to pass a quiet winter.

In fact, both the French and the English were relatively pleased with events on the Western Front that fall. And it was true that much had gone well. The French had mobilized five million men and moved them up by train or truck to battle stations; the British had been able to send four divisions across the Channel in four weeks—all without the slightest hindrance from the enemy. These facts added up, in the Allied view, to a spectacular feat of arms—at a meager price. "In 1914," ran one French boast, "we suffered 100,000 killed during the first four months. This time we have lost only 2,000." And those casualties were from accidents and minor patrol skirmishes.

Added to these accomplishments was a Royal Navy blockade designed to halt the flow of seaborne supplies to the enemy and lead to the economic strangulation of Germany. The prevailing opinion of the Allied leaders, as expressed by Oliver Harvey of the British Foreign Office, was that "if Germany cannot win a quick success, she cannot hope to win a long-drawn war." The only hope of a quick success for the Germans—so Allied leaders believed—would have been to smash into France before the French and British armies were ready to take the blow. Now that they were in place behind their fortifications, the Allies reasoned, that hope was gone.

Yet beneath this mood of self-congratulation there was some early uneasiness—and with good reason. The British and French governments were still headed by Neville Chamberlain and Edouard Daladier, the very men who had, albeit reluctantly, sold out their Czechoslovakian ally at Munich. They were hardly the men calculated to arouse popular enthusiasm, or to give people a clear idea of what they might be fighting for. Nor did they do either one of those things. Neither the French nor the British peoples were the least bit enthusiastic about this war. They watched their young men

A LUXURY LINER'S MASTERFUL END RUN

In late August, 1939, the German liner *Bremen* lay in New York Harbor ready but unable to sail for home. The British had asked the United States to delay the ship —a rich prize in the event of war—long enough for a Royal Navy cruiser to position itself in nearby American waters. In response, U.S. port officials trumped up a keel-to-masthead inspection.

By August 30, the cruiser was on station and the *Bremen* sailed, her band defiantly playing "*Deutschland über Alles.*" Whereupon she simply vanished onto the broad Atlantic. For weeks thereafter, while the blitzkrieg raged across Poland, the ship's fate was unknown. Had she been sunk with all hands by a warship?

The answer came in mid-October when the ship's Dutch cook showed up in Amsterdam with a tale of skillful blockade running. After two days at sea, playing hide-and-seek with the cruiser, the speedy liner had poured on the coal, turned north and run around the British end, while her crew camouflaged her sleek black sides with gray paint (*right*). On September 6, she arrived at the then friendly Russian port of Murmansk. All but a skeleton crew traveled overland back to Germany; the *Bremen* sneaked along the Scandinavian coast and got home in December 1939.

Crewmen suspended outside the ship's rails in lifeboats paint the Bremen's sides a drab shade to help conceal the vessel from British patrols.

go off—in many cases resignedly, if not sullenly—to the front. They looked fearfully at the skies, expecting a hail of bombs to destroy their cities. Women and children were evacuated from the major cities. But no bombs came, and the people slowly dribbled back when nothing happened.

By mid-October, nothing much seemed to be happening anywhere. General Maurice Gamelin, the French commander-in-chief, sent a few token patrols into Germany—he called it "leaning against the Siegfried Line," but they were soon called back. Occasionally there was a dogfight among fighter planes. British night bombers dropped millions of pamphlets over Germany telling the Germans that their leaders were racketeers, barbarians and losers, that "The Democracies are fighting your fight," and that "England's fleet is strangling the war apparatus of the Nazi dictatorship." The Germans boomed back with band music and propaganda speeches from loudspeakers placed in the no man's land between the Maginot and the Siegfried lines.

From "a reliable officer on leave" from the French Army, one correspondent obtained a particularly amusing sidelight on the period. The officer was "stationed just at the point where France, Germany and Luxembourg join; and it appears that at this point there were twin villages on either side of the frontier. The electric light plant for these villages was on the German side and the Germans cut the current. The French promptly shelled the German village. After several hours, the current came on again. The shelling ceased."

Some time afterward, the current stopped again. "But not 10 minutes passed before a German loud-speaker went into action. 'Please restrain your fire,' said a voice in French. 'The cutting of the current is due, not to political, but to purely technical reasons.' " The French, "roaring with laughter," did hold their fire; "and sure enough, within two hours, the French troops were enjoying free German electricity."

French courtesy matched German politeness in another incident near Mulhouse. When the French decided to blow up a steel footbridge over the Rhine, they carefully warned the Germans in advance.

There had never been a war quite like this one. The French called it "drôle de guerre," or "odd war"; Neville Chamberlain called it "a twilight war"; and Americans soon came to call it "the phony war."

Only at sea did anybody really fight and die. German submarines had sunk the British liner *Athenia* (though Berlin promptly denied responsibility) at the very start of the war, and a few days later a German U-boat commanded by Lieutenant Günther Prien, in one of the most daring exploits of the war, had slipped into the main anchorage of the British fleet at Scapa Flow in the Orkneys and had sunk the British battleship *Royal Oak*. Other U-boats and surface raiders like the pocket battleship *Graf Spee* sank a number of merchant ships, but not enough of them to seriously threaten Britain's lifelines. And the *Graf Spee* was eventually trapped in South American waters and scuttled. For lack of land action of any sort, these incidents made big headlines, but they were only minor incidents in the developing conflict.

The British were willing, if not anxious, to fight to get rid of Hitler, but they had no sizable army to speak of. They had barely started to rearm, and the four divisions—two of them undertrained and underequipped—that were all they had to offer at the start made only a drop in the ocean of French manpower. The French, possessing what many experts still regarded as the finest fighting force in the world, had never really recovered from the trauma of World War I. Buffeted by defeatist propaganda, on the one hand from the Communists who had become pacifists immediately after the Nazi-Soviet pact, and on the other from pro-Nazi reactionaries, they were divided and dispirited.

In addition they held their leaders in continuing, bitter disrespect. Lucien Rebattet, a young French Right-Winger, wrote with deep irony: "I do not feel the least anger against Hitler, but much against all the French politicians who have led to his triumph."

About the only point on which the French people and their politicians agreed was a bone-deep mistrust of the perfidious British. After all, the islands of the British homeland were protected not only by the panzer-proof Channel but by the Royal Navy; clearly the English intended to limit their activities to the sea and air, and would let the French poilus fill up the casualty lists on hand. Alexis Léger of the French Foreign Ministry told American Ambassador William Bullitt: "The game is lost. France stands alone. . . . The Democracies are again too late."

Daladier himself told Bullitt that he had come to the conclusion that Britain meant France to fight the War alone.

French officers often treated their brothers-in-arms from across the Channel with a condescension bordering on contempt. When General Gamelin, who was named Supreme Commander of the Allied ground forces in Europe, held his first staff meeting with the British generals in order to explain what he wanted to do, he did not even bother to have an interpreter along. He talked so rapidly and so peremptorily in his native tongue that not half of his words were understood by his British listeners.

Meanwhile French morale was sinking, not only among civilians but in the Army too. General Edmond Ruby of the Second Army complained of "a general apathy and ignorance among the ranks. No one dared to give an order for fear of being criticized. Military exercises were considered a joke, and work unnecessary drudgery." Some officers, including Colonel de Gaulle, urgently recommended that the troops be trained intensively not only to prepare them for battle but also to lift their flagging spirits. Hampered by an archaic and inefficient command structure, the activists got

nowhere. Ruby noted that only half a day per week was set aside for training. Ruby was also concerned by the effect of boredom upon the troops. "Drunkenness had made an immediate appearance and in the larger railway stations special rooms had to be set up to cope with it—euphemistically known as de-ethylization rooms."

British troops, who were all spit-and-polish, were appalled by the carelessness, even outright sloppiness, of the French troops that they encountered. General Alan Brooke, the commander of the II Corps of the British Expeditionary Force, was invited to a military ceremony by General André-Georges Corap, the commander of the French Ninth Army. "Seldom," Brooke wrote, "have I seen anything more slovenly and badly turned out. Men unshaven, horses ungroomed, clothes and saddlery that did not fit, vehicles dirty, and complete lack of pride in themselves and their units. What shook me most . . . was the look in the men's faces, disgruntled and insubordinate looks, and although ordered to give 'Eyes left,' hardly a man bothered to do so."

Nor were the British very much impressed by General Gamelin, even though some of the Germans entertained a degree of respect for him. "A nice old man," said Sir John Slessor of the British Air Ministry, "not remotely equal to his enormous job." Nevertheless, the British generals were determined not to repeat the organizational errors of the First World War, when it took four years to get a unified command of the French and British under Marshal Foch, and therefore, despite their misgivings, they accepted all of General Gamelin's orders.

The Allied armies ultimately might have fared better had the British been less accommodating. For basically, Gamelin's system of operations made no sense, and it is hard to understand why no one on the highest levels of power at the time seemed to notice it. He kept a small headquarters team with him in the ancient fortress of Vincennes near Paris. "There he was," recalled de Gaulle, "in a setting which recalled a convent, attended by a few officers, working and meditating without mixing in day-to-day duties. In his *thébaïde* [retreat] at Vincennes, General Gamelin gave the impression of a savant, testing the chemical reactions of his strategy in a laboratory."

Poring over his maps and mountains of reports like an el-derly professor, Gamelin paid little or no attention to the need for effective means of staying in touch with his key subordinates' command posts. Communications between his "submarine without a periscope" (as another officer called it) and other headquarters posts had to go through the civilian telegraph and long-distance telephone facilities. Then as now, these lines were not noted for their efficiency. The alternate method of staying in touch was via motorcycle couriers, who under wartime conditions were as likely as not to end up in a ditch.

On more or less suitable occasions, the Allied commanders got together over gargantuan lunches; for example, the one that is recorded in General Brooke's diary for October 31, 1939: "Oysters, lobsters, chicken, pâté de foie gras, pheasant, cheese and fruit, coffee, liqueurs, etc." And on November 2: "Again a heavy lunch, with hors d'oeuvres, trout, duck and mushrooms, cheese, ices, fruits, coffee and liqueurs! I hope this is the last of these lunches; they interfere with my work and my liver."

On the home front on the Allied side, meanwhile, life continued to be a bizarre mixture of excitement and foreboding —a paradox produced by patriotic saber-rattling, boredom at the business-as-usual reality of so much of the Phony War,

fatigue from the extra work effort necessary for hurried rearming and endless rumor-swapping. In Britain, among the more widely circulated rumors were these:

• That the BEF was on the point of leaving France because "the war is really over."
• That Hitler had imported 30,000 gorillas from Brazil to be trained for an immediate attack on the Maginot Line.
• That the government was adulterating margarine with cat fat and permitting restaurants to put cat meat in steak-and-kidney pie, a British staple.
• That peace was being arranged so that Britain, France and Germany could combine for an attack on the Soviet Union.
• That the Russians had a device on their parachutes that could propel a paratrooper or a downed flyer back into the air again if he didn't like the spot he was about to land on.
• That the first great German air raid on Britain was scheduled for next week—probably Tuesday.

In France, there was still no rationing of food or fuel, and troublesome regulations like the blackout of cities and roads were not taken seriously after the first few days of false alarms. A German plane flying over France could have been led straight to Paris on a Friday or a Sunday night by the endless lines of cars with their headlights on, taking prosperous Parisians out to or back from their customary weekends in the country. The Paris fashion house of Molyneux trotted out its fall collection as usual, although only 40 models paraded instead of the normal 200. To remind other spectators at the opening that there was a war on, a Mrs. Reginald Fellowes, over from England, knitted socks for soldiers while the models pranced.

The fashionable restaurants of Paris were crowded every night with politicians and would-be politicians and their lady friends discussing the burning questions of the hour: How long could the bovine Daladier survive as prime minister? Was it true that Hitler had blown his brains out in a fit of nervous depression? How many German spies were working in the Foreign Ministry? But scarcely anybody raised the one important question: What would happen if the German Army pierced the Maginot Line?

Of all those responsible for addressing this latter question, the Allied High Command seemed the least concerned. Convinced of their invulnerability in the west, the generals spent precious days and weeks contentedly spinning out more or less fanciful plans for surprise assaults against Germany's distant flanks or rear.

One possible target was Italy, closest at hand, and an ally of Germany under the "Pact of Steel" signed by Hitler and Mussolini in May 1939. An Allied offensive aimed at the Italians might have stood a good chance of success. In fact the French Army had long before laid contingency plans for an invasion of Italy. Though the passes over the Alps were relatively easy to defend, Mussolini had little with which to hold them. The Italians, despite years of bluster by the Duce, had never built up a modern army. Some of the Italian units were well trained and effective, but most of them were made up of second-rate troops, poorly armed and poorly fed, with only a limited industrial base to keep them supplied. A joke around German headquarters in those days was that Hitler asked a German general what would have to be done if Italy entered the War. "If Italy is against us," said the general, "we will need five divisions to hold the passes over the Alps; if they come in on our side, we will have to send them 27 divisions to give them some backbone."

For the time being, Mussolini had neatly side-stepped any danger—and had conveniently ignored his agreement with Hitler—by hastily declaring Italy to be a nonbelligerent in September 1939. The French and British had, naturally, welcomed this decision and had let Mussolini's Italy alone in the succeeding months. They preferred to plan hazy descents on far more distant or more difficult areas: Scandinavia, the Balkans, even the Caucasus.

In pursuit of this last will-o-the-wisp, the French assembled an army in Syria under the command of General Maxime Weygand, Marshal Foch's chief of staff in 1918. This Middle East force, in large part composed of colonial units, was not so much a unified body as it was an agglomeration of 40,000 men supported by neither tanks nor planes. The French had a vague scheme for employing the Syrian contingent to cut off Hitler's supplies of oil from the Russian fields, although how they expected to get to the oil fields over hundreds of miles of virtually roadless mountains and deserts against determined Soviet resistance was never made clear. One disenchanted British general referred to the Allied strategists of this period as "The Crazy Gang," after a troupe of comedians on the BBC.

Major Emile Speller (right), chief of the Luxembourg Army, reviews a good portion of his command in a snowy courtyard in the capital. During the winter of 1940, the Grand Duchy's defense force consisted of 400 infantrymen and a 12-horse cavalry troop to oppose the mechanized German divisions massed along the border. Nonetheless, the nominally neutral Luxembourgers intrepidly mounted what they called a "passive defense" of their tiny country. To back up the army, they erected barbed-wire barricades on frontier roads, closed bridges across the Duchy's river border with Germany and evacuated its border towns.

Only one aspect of the strategic theorizing indulged in by the Allied generals had real substance. That was the part dealing with the possibilities of imminent German attack from the west. In preparation for this eventuality, the French military planners originally had assumed that the Germans would not think of a direct assault on the formidable barrier of the Maginot Line, with its well-sited underground forts a quarter to a half mile apart along the Franco-German frontier. A more likely alternative, they reasoned, would be a sweep by an overwhelming mass of troops through the Low Countries into France.

In meeting this thrust, one choice would be to mass the French and British forces on the Franco-Belgian frontier and receive the shock of the German offensive there. This was the simplest course of action, but it could just as easily be self-defeating. The heavily fortified Maginot Line faced Germany only. Its extension along the Franco-Belgian border to the Channel—sometimes called the Little Maginot Line—consisted only of scattered defenses with little depth. Behind this shaky barrier lay one of France's major industrial areas, the loss of which would be crippling. However, the Belgians had fortified their frontier with Germany strongly, and it should have been possible to hold these fortifications, by shoring them up so they became, in effect, a northern extension of the Maginot Line. It was therefore decided to back up this line by moving large numbers of Allied troops rapidly into Belgium at the moment of the German advance. As it turned out, this decision—logical as it may have seemed at the time—was fatally mistaken (page 117).

As the staffs on both sides toiled into the early winter, the war plans of the Allies and the Germans began to shape a massive battle of confrontation. Both intended to throw the bulk of their forces into the north Belgian plain. And if Hitler had had his way and had been able to get started early, the two armies would have collided head on in open country in the midst of the worst weather Europe had seen for 50 years. The German planes, the one arm in which the Nazis had decisive superiority, would have been grounded most of the time. Hitler's forces might well have won the tank battle, because of the superior organization, training and tactics of the German panzer divisions. But the casualties would surely have been enormous and the chances for a decisive German breakthrough small.

Meanwhile, having been unable to launch his attack before the worst of winter set in, Hitler suddenly decided just at the end of the year to augment his projected campaign in western Europe with an attack on the Scandinavian countries, a move that would protect his northern flank—and more importantly, would give him unimpeded access to raw materials in the area. His idea was to use small, mobile forces including parachute troops and light naval units that would not be missed on the Western Front.

Then came the plane crash at Mechelen-sur-Meuse, delivering parts of the German attack plan to the Allies and giving them the heaven-sent chance to exploit the Germans' disarray after a potentially disastrous check to their plans.

Although the Allies rushed troops to the Franco-Belgian border in a show of strength, they did no more than that. They complacently left their own plans firmly intact—and missed the opportunity to catch Hitler off balance.

He was not off balance for long. After recovering from his hysteria over the crash, he coolly investigated his alternatives. He toyed for a while with the idea of stepping up the date of the attack and going ahead with it anyway. But alarming reports from the meteorologists forced yet another postponement, this time until spring.

Thus, Hitler was open to new proposals. He had never been fully satisfied with his generals' plans for the campaign against the Low Countries anyway, and now he was forced by circumstance into reevaluating them. In fact he was well along in doing so. Despite Brauchitsch's earlier doubts about attacking through the Ardennes against the strategic city of Sedan—the hinge between the Maginot and Little Maginot lines—the Führer had insisted that a panzer corps be prepared to do just that.

Hitler had little patience with the conventional military view of the Ardennes as too heavily wooded and too rough in terrain to permit a tank attack. His impatience was well founded. The fact was that much of the region was ideal tank country, with wide fields and good roads; and as for the forests, they offered a perfect cover for camouflaging entire divisions of tanks from air observation. Indeed, the French Army, on maneuvers in 1938, had actually staged a mock attack on Sedan through the area; the exercise involved seven "German" divisions, supported by tanks, which smashed through the Ardennes and routed the defense.

Whether or not Hitler or any of his generals knew about this French war game, a few German officers were convinced that the region was actually suited to the deployment of a much larger force than the one Hitler had in mind. The most articulate of these officers was General Erich von Manstein, then chief of staff to General Gerd von Rundstedt's Army Group A, which was to be in charge of any thrust on Sedan.

In a steady barrage of memoranda, which Rundstedt fully endorsed and sent along to the Wehrmacht's Supreme Headquarters, Manstein—with the further support of Guderian—argued that even the revised plans were hopelessly inadequate because they looked forward to winning only a battle, which might well end in a stalemate like that of 1914-1918. As the Army Group A officers saw it, the object was to destroy the Anglo-French forces in a massive, decisive stroke. This stroke he wanted just where Hitler had proposed his relatively small panzer strike, through the Ardennes. But instead of sending a single armored corps, Manstein would strike with the principal weight of the Army Group A.

By this new scenario, the originally planned German attack through the Low Countries would be only a feint to draw the Allies into advancing in the wrong direction. And while the enemy was plunging on to the north, the German *Sichelschnitt*—scythe-cut—in the south would slice right through to the sea and catch the bulk of the Allied armies in a gigantic trap.

Persuasive though they were, none of the proposals developed by Rundstedt and Manstein reached Hitler. Nevertheless, their steady pressure on Brauchitsch and Halder slowly took effect. With the January postponement of the offensive, Army Group A increased its urging that the decisive thrust be shifted southward.

And because Hitler himself increasingly doubted the effectiveness of the old plan, on February 13 he ordered his general staff to study the question of changing the focus of the attack and launching a tank assault against Sedan where it would not be expected.

At this crucial point a routine ceremony brought Manstein to see the Führer. Manstein, long due for field duty, had been transferred from the staff to an infantry corps command, a job that involved control of as many as 60,000 men. As was his custom when generals were posted to a new and higher command, Hitler received at dinner, on February 17 in Berlin, five new corps commanders, one of whom was Manstein. The right talker had found the right listener. Manstein gave a detailed, thoroughly professional outline of his plan, and Hitler was delighted. This was what he had been waiting for; it fitted in with his own thinking, and with the study he had ordered his High Command to undertake.

At noon on the very next day Halder came to see Hitler with the latest general-staff plan for the offensive. It incorporated all the essentials of the Manstein-Rundstedt plan, while considerably strengthening them. The bombardment of memoranda from Group A had had its effect on the High Command. And after the new directive from Hitler, Halder and his staff had come up with a yet more radical concept —though Halder had the gall to say that Manstein's suggestions had been his own ideas from the very start. Full of enthusiasm after his meeting with Manstein, impressed with Halder's development of the new plan, Hitler threw his energy and ingenuity into refining it. For the next few days he and his generals worked furiously, and by February 24 it was in final shape. The attack was scheduled for May.

On the Allied side, meanwhile, the British Expeditionary Force on the Franco-Belgian frontier in April of 1940 still consisted of no more than 10 divisions, less than 400,000 men, and one tank brigade. The Belgians persisted in their refusal to cooperate with the Allies, fearing that doing so would compromise their neutrality. Churchill, as First Lord of the Admiralty, was advocating action at sea and in the air, and criticizing Chamberlain for his lack of initiative. Paul Reynaud, who had become Premier of France in March, after the fall of the Daladier government for its failure to act, made confident speeches proclaiming that: "We shall win, because we are strongest."

When Hitler had definitely set the attack on Belgium, Holland and Luxembourg for May 10—and a second German force was already embarked to invade Scandinavia—the Allied leaders stubbornly continued to assume that Hitler had lost his chance for a successful offensive in the west by not attacking immediately after the fall of Poland, while the British and French were unprepared. Their attitude was summed up in the deluded phrase of Neville Chamberlain, who declared on April 5, in a speech to fellow Tories, that Hitler had "missed the bus."

FROLIC ON THE WESTERN FRONT

A squad of British Tommies with fixed bayonets attacks a platoon of turkeys by a French barnyard gate in anticipation of their 1939 Christmas dinner.

ALL DRESSED UP BUT NO WAR TO FIGHT

In Berlin, the 1939-1940 blackout had amenities: at a subway stop, a volunteer escort offers to conduct a late shopper safely to her front door.

Following the swift, bloody conquest of Poland in September 1939, Germany turned to face the French and British armies, drawn up along the Reich's border with France. There the men on both sides found themselves coping with an odd but welcome paradox: the War, though declared, was not really in effect. No tanks crashed against the elaborate defenses of France's Maginot Line; no shells dropped on Germany's Siegfried Line across the Rhine, no planes buzzed overhead. In fact, hardly a shot was fired in anger on the Western Front during the entire winter of 1939-1940.

Both sides did their best to adjust to this parody of war. In the British homeland, the gentry, anxious to offer a gesture of involvement, made room in their homes for hospital beds and War Office desks. City dwellers groped through blackouts that raised mild complaints from British wives unable to fetch the old man's dinner in the dark; French and German women complained they were afraid of molesters.

For the men, adjustment often meant a new life in the military; husbands and sons, servants and office workers marched off to join the colors. The call-up took thousands of Britishers and Frenchmen off to chilly posts on the French frontier. German soldiers, already mobilized and blooded in Poland, faced them across the Rhine as both sides waited for attack orders that never seemed to come.

Meanwhile, the war spewed out a deluge of words. The Germans mounted a propaganda campaign that exploited French soldiers' disgruntlement at leaving home and family. Leaflets and loud-speakers told them that while the British sent over machines, Frenchmen were being asked to die.

The bored troops endured military routine ranging from close-order drill to fingernail inspection, and they entertained themselves as best they could. British officers kept in trim with early morning walks. Poilus—the stubble-faced French common soldiers—raised rabbits and shivered in unusually severe winter weather. And, as French sentries watched their German counterparts across the lines, there seemed little point in shooting. "After all," said one, "they aren't bad types, and if we fire, they will fire back."

In England, Lady Juliet Duff poses on wartime transportation before windows papered for blackout. Her chauffeur (right) and butler were both in the Army.

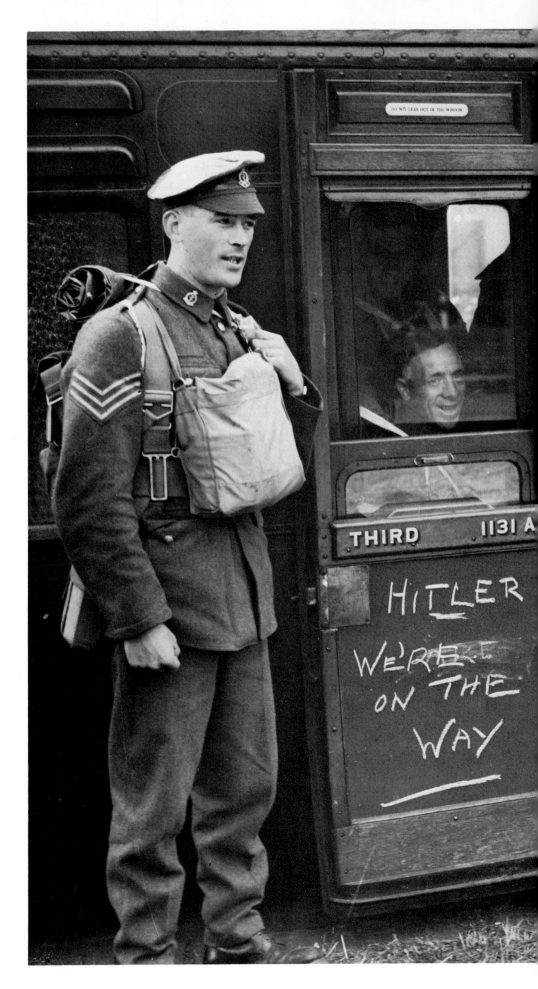

A mandolin-playing corporal of the Royal Army Medical Corps leads his buddies in a rendition of "We're Gonna Hang Out the Washing on the Siegfried Line"—a musical boast predicting the quick collapse of the vaunted defense system along Germany's western borders. Self-conscious and cheerful, British Tommies like these members of a British Expeditionary Force leaving for Belgium and France gave the impression that they were off for an easy replay of their fathers' roles in World War I.

Opposite the French Maginot Line somewhere near Strasbourg, a German army band oompahs its way through a selection of 1940 French popular favorites. The event was part of an organized Wehrmacht effort to recast the image of the German soldier from a rapacious Hun to a jolly neighbor who would not dream of attacking anybody.

A German soldier sets up a loud-speaker to beam a mixture of music and propaganda at bored French poilus in positions only a few hundred yards away. Even the most passionate Gallic patriots agreed that the Wehrmacht broadcasts were much more entertaining than the super-patriotic official French programs.

Propaganda leaflets tied to balloons are prepared for take-off from the Siegfried Line. The leaflets contained antiwar slogans and hints about straying wives and unfaithful sweethearts—all calculated to convince even the toughest poilu that there were more important things in life than shooting Germans.

A sign set up on the German front lines along the Rhine, in clear view of the opposing French, reads: "The German people won't attack the French people, if the French don't attack the Germans." In the spirit of the message, French soldiers refrained from firing on Germans who were carrying on such propagandizing.

A French peasant in his cart pulls over as the General Staff of the British Expeditionary Force, led by General Viscount Gort, takes its daily constitutional.

Maintaining strict peacetime garrison routine, a French hygiene officer puts newly recruited cooks through a fingernail inspection.

A relaxed poilu on sentry duty sits out his shift in an orchard with his Chatellerault M29 light machine gun propped at his side.

Brigadier General Adolphe François Vieillard, a French infantry commander, lifts a glass of Christmas champagne with his officers and men near a front-line bunker that was disguised as a woodshed. The champagne needed no chilling; that year the winter on the quiet Western Front was the coldest in a half century.

3

On February 5, 1940, a meeting of the Allied Supreme Command—the top military and civilian brass of Britain and France—was marked by an unusual accord. "Everyone was purring," noted British General Sir Edmund Ironside, Chief of the Imperial General Staff. The Allied leaders had reached agreement on sending an expeditionary force across the North Sea to invade two neutral nations—Norway and Sweden—and were delighted with their plan: It gave them a chance to deliver a flanking blow to Hitler and cripple Germany's armament industry at very little cost to themselves.

They would have been infinitely less pleased if they had known that Hitler was thinking along similar lines and laying detailed plans that would lead to a grim encounter in Norway. But the elation of the Allied planners was unaffected by any such knowledge, though their enthusiasm was not shared by those further down the line who would have to deal with the practical problems of the Scandinavian adventure. At the headquarters of the British Expeditionary Force in France, where field leaders were desperately trying to build up a respectable fighting force, there was incredulity and dismay when the staff learned that two whole divisions that had been earmarked for France with all their invaluable equipment were now to be sent off to chase wild geese in the far north. General Henry Pownall, the BEF's Chief of Staff, made this furious entry in his diary: "For five months we have been struggling to make fit for action in the spring a force that last September was dangerously under-equipped and untrained. . . . There were signs that we were getting some reasonable way to our goal. . . . If this business goes through (and the saving grace is that I don't believe it can) we shall be cut by 30 per cent. It is a most disheartening business. . . . Of all the harebrained projects I have heard of, this is the most foolish."

The original author of the project was none other than Winston Churchill. Upon his appointment as First Lord of the Admiralty in September 1939, Churchill had immediately begun looking for a way to outflank the enemy. His restless eye soon lighted on the coast of Norway. Here was a thousand miles of fjord and headland, which according to some authorities constituted Germany's economic lifeline.

A considerable percentage, perhaps almost half, of the iron that Germany needed to make steel for its guns, tanks and ships came from a mining complex around Kiruna and

IRON HANDS ON SCANDINAVIA

Gällivare in northern Sweden. About 20 per cent of this ore went to Germany from the Swedish port of Luleå on the Gulf of Bothnia, during the six to seven months of the year when the gulf was not locked in winter ice. The other 80 per cent was shipped westward by rail over a spine of mountains to the Norwegian port of Narvik, whose Gulf Stream-warmed waters are ice-free all year round. Vessels loading ore there could evade the British blockade on their way to Germany by staying within neutral Norwegian waters—within three miles of that country's long coast.

Churchill was convinced that, by cutting off this Narvik traffic, Britain could strike a telling blow against the Nazi war industry. It was an alluring prospect and Churchill, characteristically, wanted to move at once. However, in September 1939 he was not yet the all-powerful figure he later became in Britain. His proposals were referred to and debated by committees—British committees, French committees, inter-Allied committees, military staffs, economic staffs, diplomatic staffs. And the days and weeks went by as quibbles arose and papers were shuffled.

The committees had, it is true, a great deal to quibble about. One Churchill plan called for British warships to cut off the Narvik ore traffic by laying minefields in Norwegian territorial waters. But for any such action, the Allies needed the assent of the neutral Norwegians and Swedes, which was not easy to obtain. Alternately Mr. Churchill thought Britain might undertake to paralyze most of the available shipping by chartering away the enormous Norwegian ore-boat fleet. In either case, he noted, the Allies might do well to indemnify Sweden for the loss of her German market by purchasing the ore themselves. "It is far from our wish," declared Churchill, "to quarrel with the Swedes."

Or with the Norwegians, for that matter; any quarrel with either Sweden or Norway would destroy all Allied hope of their cooperation. And without such cooperation, an Allied move to block the ore shipments could degenerate into a sticky violation of Scandinavian neutrality.

While these awkward matters were being debated in London and Paris following the First Lord's initial proposal to put a crimp in the ore traffic, events in Scandinavia introduced a whole new set of terms into the strategic and diplomatic equation. On November 30, Russia attacked its small neighbor, Finland. This apparently impulsive step by Stalin was actually the climax of a series of moves he had begun the moment most of the Baltic area had been recognized as his sphere of influence under the Nazi-Soviet treaty.

His tactic had been to invite the heads of Latvia, Lithuania and Estonia to Moscow, overwhelm them with caviar and vodka and evenings at the ballet, and then present an ultimatum: Give the Red Army and Navy bases on your territory, or else. The visitors were in no position to challenge what the "else" might mean; their countries were small and helpless, and so they signed up quickly. Then, early in October, Stalin felt it was the turn of the Finns to make territorial concessions to the Soviet Union.

The Finns, however, proved unexpectedly stubborn. Instead of instantly capitulating as others had, they attempted to bargain. Negotiations dragged on until Stalin lost patience. On November 26, Soviet Foreign Minister Vyacheslav Molotov called in the Finnish Ambassador to Moscow and handed him a note accusing the Finns of directing artillery fire at the Soviet village of Mainila on the Karelian Isthmus, killing four Red Army soldiers and wounding nine. This, declared Molotov, was "provocational shelling."

Then, according to the Russians, Finnish soldiers crossed the Russian border during the early dawn hours of November 30. At 8 a.m., in response to this alleged aggression, the Red Army launched an all-out land, sea and air attack against Finland. Thirty divisions and six tank brigades rolled across the Finnish border; bombers and fighters roared over Helsinki and other major Finnish cities from new Russian bases in Estonian territory.

Bombers aiming at targets such as railroad stations, freight yards, power plants and piers managed to drop their cargoes in residential areas, causing considerable loss of civilian life. Finnish reports of these air raids were dismissed as fabrications by the Soviet radio, which claimed that the Russian Air Force had been dropping not bombs but bread to Finland's starving masses. The Finns smiled wryly as they fought the fires started by the Russian incendiaries, and dubbed the Soviet bombs "Molotov's breadbaskets."

The world was at first shocked by the Soviet assault on inoffensive Finland, and then amazed. Contrary to all expectation, the Finns soon had the Russians staggering, if not on their knees. It turned out that the Soviet troops were inadequately equipped for a war in the fast-approaching Arctic winter. Moreover, they were wretchedly led, mainly because a large part of their officer corps had been shot by Stalin's secret police during purges of the late 1930s. Also, the Finnish terrain—heavy forest and tundra dotted with innumerable lakes—was very difficult to attack through. Above all, the Russians themselves were grossly overconfident; Stalin appears to have thought that the Finns, confronted by massive strength, would simply roll over and quit.

He was badly mistaken. The Finns had a tough little ground army of 300,000 men, who fought back with an ingenuity far greater than their strength. Lacking antitank guns they devised an ingenious deterrent against Soviet armored units. Nicknamed the Molotov cocktail as an ironic twist on the Molotov breadbasket, this lethal apéritif was a blend of potassium chlorate and kerosene served in a bottle with a detonator at its mouth. To deliver it, a daring ski-borne soldier would ambush a Russian tank and hurl the simple but devastating grenade against the turret or engine compartment. It would burst into flame on contact, disabling the vehicle and routing the crew.

In the face of such unexpected toughness—and the unrelenting bite of the Arctic wind—Russian units huddled half-starved and half-frozen in the snowdrifts, to be annihilated group by group. Whole Soviet divisions disappeared in this manner, cut down in bivouac. Hidden Finnish machine gunners decimated columns of Red soldiers slogging through the snow. Often the fallen bodies froze stiff within minutes. Correspondent Leland Stowe of the Chicago *Daily News* wrote eloquently of the corpses strewn along a roadway. "In this sad solitude lie the dead," he reported, "uncounted thousands of Russian dead. They lie as they fell—twisted, gesticulating and tortured . . . beneath a kindly mask of two inches of new-fallen snow."

Even though the Russians had some 2,500 planes to let loose on Finland, and though they dropped about 150,000 explosive and incendiary bombs on the country in the course of the winter, Finnish civilians remained as calm and confident as the troops at the front. One American journalist reported that a maid in his hotel would, upon hearing the air raid sirens, carol out her heavily accented English phrase, "Molotov is here!" and go placidly about her business.

The heroic resistance of the Finns and the wretched performance of the Russians stirred a good deal of enthusiasm and support for the Finnish cause throughout the West. Sweden sent substantial quantities of war matériel, including 25 planes, 104 antiaircraft guns, 84,000 rifles with 50 million rounds of ammunition, 85 antitank guns, and 112 field guns and howitzers. Eight thousand Swedish volunteers sped to the Finnish front. In addition, the Swedes raised $100 million, largely by popular subscription, to provide Finland with medical supplies, clothing, food and other goods. The United States offered a $30 million loan with the proviso that it be used only for civilian purchases, and placed an embargo on the sale of military materials to the Soviet Union. Great Britain and France promised to send technicians, planes and weapons to Finland; Denmark and Norway permitted volunteers to offer their services.

Though Germany had helped the Finns in their war against the Communists 20 years before, Hitler decided this time to do nothing. He needed the raw materials such as grain and oil that he was getting in wholesale quantities from Russia, and he needed Russia's benevolent neutrality so that he could have a free hand when he was ready to attack in the west. At the same time he was not averse to seeing the Soviet Union set back, and as he followed the fighting in Finland he formed dangerously erroneous ideas about the capabilities of the Red Army. Wipert von Blücher, the German minister at Helsinki, did much to reinforce these disparaging judgments. On January 11 he reported—accurately—that the Red Army was suffering defeat upon defeat in spite of its superior manpower and equipment.

Then he added with some enthusiasm: "In view of this experience, ideas on Bolshevist Russia must be thoroughly revised. All of us started with the wrong premises when we assumed that Russia was a first-rate military factor. . . . The experience gained in Finland shows that Russia has not for some time past constituted a threat to the great power, Germany. In these circumstances it might now be possible to adopt an entirely different tone toward the gentlemen in the Kremlin from that of August and September."

This delusion was shared by the British and the French. In a broadcast of January 20, Churchill, still in his cabinet post, told the British public that the winter war "had exposed, for the world to see, the military incapacity of the Red Army." What the First Lord did not say out loud was that Stalin's ap-

Finland's Field Marshal Carl Gustav von Mannerheim, an aristocratic soldier, under whose command a small force fought Stalin's Red Army to a temporary standstill, stands proudly beside game trophies on a stairway of his Finnish castle. In addition to his military skills, Mannerheim was an accomplished sportsman and explorer who hunted stags in Germany, antelope and man-eating tigers in Nepal, and was the first European to explore and chart portions of Siberia's remote Arctic.

parent blunder had presented the Allies with a solid gold pretext for launching Churchill's ultimate measure. Obviously the humanitarian thing to do was to send large armed units to help the beleaguered Finns; and anyone could see that the only practical route to that hapless country lay through northern Norway and Sweden. On their way to Finland, obviously, the Allied troops would overrun the iron mines at Kiruna and Gällivare. And thus Germany would be deprived of that vital ore. The specific plan Churchill recommended called for the Allies to land at Narvik, follow the railroad into Sweden and set up a base at Luleå. When that position was consolidated, one brigade would move into Finland while two held the Narvik-Luleå area. At the conference of February 5, where General Ironside heard the purring, this scheme was accepted with delight by both the British and French high commands. The Allied leaders decided forthwith to prepare three or four divisions, starting with the two British divisions previously intended for France.

"An air of unreality pervades the proceedings of this conference," noted one frank observer. And this lack of reality about a Scandinavian coup extended not just to using troops and equipment that were urgently needed elsewhere. It also included "underestimation of the administrative difficulties of such a campaign, the slight regard paid to the danger of provoking Soviet hostility, the miscalculation of German efficiency and resource, and the wishful thinking, which discounted the determination of the neutral governments to maintain their neutrality."

And that wasn't all. The proposed campaign, due to start March 20, might well have brought Germany into the Finnish conflict on Russia's side and turned Finland into a battleground for the great powers. Fortunately, however, it never took place. Before the Allied divisions were even marshaled for embarkation, Russia removed the pretext for the scheme by crushing Finland—as everyone had expected them to do far earlier. On February 1, tremendous artillery barrages broke over the Finnish lines in the Karelian Isthmus, the narrow strip of land between Lake Ladoga and the Gulf of Finland. Behind them a crushing force of infantry and tanks under tough new commanders surged over the Finns, who did not have enough men or bullets to stop them.

By early March it was all over, and a humiliated Finnish peace delegation to Moscow was forced to give Stalin more land than he had originally demanded. Included in the new package was Viipuri, their second largest city. "The territory ceded amounted to 16,000 square miles," said Finland's Commander-in-Chief, Field Marshal Carl Gustav von Mannerheim, "and its inhabitants formed 12 per cent of the population of the country." It was a devastating loss for the Finns, who had defended their territory inch by bloody inch in the months of fighting.

It was also a devastating surprise to the Allies. All the ambitious plans of the Supreme Command seemed now to add up to zero. The Finnish capitulation even brought about the downfall of the Daladier government in France, where the electorate was wholly out of patience with the official failure to help Finland—or to prosecute any other part of the War. Daladier was succeeded by Paul Reynaud, who was installed with a mandate to take action.

But what? And where? Reynaud (with a prod or two from

Churchill) turned his eyes right back on Scandinavia. Never mind that the collapse of Finland had deprived the Allies of their best excuse for action in that sector. The ice in the Gulf of Bothnia was about to melt; for the ensuing six months, Germany would be able to ship iron out of Luleå. And meanwhile the port of Narvik in Norway was still sending out ore to the Germans. The temptation to cut the "Road of Iron" remained too big to resist.

A new plan was therefore hastily devised: the British fleet, on April 5, would lay minefields in Norwegian coastal waters that would effectively block any ore ships from getting down from Narvik to Germany. If the Germans showed any signs of retaliating in force, British and French forces would land and seize not only Narvik but also Trondheim, Bergen and Stavanger to the south—and then they would advance to the Swedish frontier.

The total force allocated to this grand design consisted of less than one division—which was to operate without air support. At this point the Allies were confident no blood would be shed, and they felt that the smaller the force, the less likelihood of a serious Norwegian protest. Once again everything was prepared in an atmosphere of enthusiasm: the Western powers were finally going to take some action and show Hitler a thing or two.

But once again, as the Allied troops were marching toward the docks, something got in their way. This time, paradoxically, it was Winston Churchill, who had come up with a brilliant counterpoint to the Scandinavian scheme. Why not, said Churchill, drop mines in the Rhine at the same time that the Scandinavian ports were being seized? That way almost all of Germany's important water traffic would be shut down at once. But the French, when consulted on this new gambit, which Churchill dubbed *Royal Marine,* developed a bad case of cold feet. Not a single German bomb had yet fallen on French soil. If the Allies started mining German rivers, might not the Luftwaffe start dropping bombs on French war factories, which were virtually defenseless owing to a shortage of antiaircraft guns? The French vetoed *Royal Marine.* And in the course of the wrangling, the Norwegian landings were postponed to April 8.

All the while they were shuffling and postponing, none of the top French and British commanders seemed to have sus-

pected that Hitler might not only be alert to the possibility of Allied interference with the Narvik ore traffic but also that he might be preparing a Scandinavian action of his own.

As it turned out, here as elsewhere in Europe thus far, Hitler was a full two steps ahead of his enemies. His naval chief, Admiral Erich Raeder, had long since presented him a report stressing the strategic importance of Norway's extended, indented coast, which was useful not only as a route for ore ships but also as a base for surface raiders and submarines then blockaded in the Baltic.

Moreover, the Führer had been receiving ambitious suggestions from a Norwegian politician named Vidkun Quisling, who was eager to promote the ideology of the Nazis in his own land—and secure for himself the top position in the new order. A brilliant graduate of Norway's War Academy, Quisling had served as military attaché in the Russian capital in 1918. He was an enthusiastic Communist sympathizer until he discovered that he had more of a future at the opposite end of the political spectrum. After making a sharp turn to the Right, he had served as Minister of Defense from 1931 to 1933, then founded a Nazi-oriented party called the Nasjonal Samling (National Union).

In various meetings with Hitler, Quisling gave dire warn-

ing of "the dangers to Germany arising from a British occupation" of Norway. Quisling then told the Führer that he was prepared to help the Germans in exchange for some financial aid. In fact, he assured Hitler that, in anticipation of a British move, he could pull off a coup in Norway and establish a Nazi-style government. Hitler was impressed enough to supply his visitor with funds to promote a pro-German movement in Norway. But as the consummate master of such intrigues, Hitler realized that no matter how vigorously Quisling went about the business of subversion, ultimately the only way to get a real hold on Norway would be through military action. And he ordered his High Command to work out a plan to occupy the entire country.

While these plans were in the making, a minor naval scuffle in Norwegian waters convinced the Führer that if he was going to strike at Norway at all, he must strike quickly. The incident focused on a peripatetic German supply ship called the *Altmark,* which had spent much of the preceding six months picking up British sailors whose ships had been sunk under them in various sea battles. With nearly 300 of these prisoners of war aboard, the *Altmark* had recently been trying to dodge her way back to Germany with a fair portion of the British Navy in pursuit. Then, on February 14, under cov-

er of fog, she reached Norwegian territorial waters.

Her arrival caused a terrible problem for the Norwegian government. Under international law, the *Altmark* had a perfect right to sail through Norway's waters—but not with prisoners of war aboard. Anxious to avoid offending Germany, the Norwegians pretended not to notice that there was anything unusual about the *Altmark*—even though the British government pointedly informed Norway about the prisoners. As a token, Norwegian officers went on board three times, ostensibly to search the ship. Despite the fact that the captives below decks were shouting and hammering with all their might, nothing was officially noticed. To the outrage of the British, the *Altmark* was not only cleared but actually given an escort of two Norwegian torpedo boats for the final jump southward to Germany.

Whereupon the British Admiralty ordered a force of six British destroyers under the command of Captain Philip Vian to intercept the German tanker. The *Altmark* was quickly sighted from the air and two British destroyers, *Ivanhoe* and *Intrepid,* were given her location and ordered to board her. Their efforts were frustrated—as much by a cautious desire to avoid a fight with the Norwegian escort vessels as by the *Altmark*'s refusal to stop. But when the *Altmark* ducked into Jösing Fjord to anchor among the ice floes, Captain Vian took the destroyer *Cossack* into the fjord and ran her up alongside the *Altmark.*

Hailing the captain of the Norwegian torpedo boat *Kjell,* Vian demanded the release of the prisoners. When the *Kjell*'s commander denied that the *Altmark* carried prisoners, Vian grappled the *Cossack* against the *Altmark*'s side and sent a boarding party swarming onto her decks.

After a brief confrontation, part of the German crew escaped to shore by swimming the bone-chilling waters of the fjord, and the rest surrendered. The British boarding party hurried belowdecks and soon found the captives locked up in storerooms and in a dry oil tank. With the cry, "The Navy's here!" the rescuers broke down the doors. The prisoners came tumbling gratefully out, debilitated by long confinement, but reasonably healthy. In the meanwhile, the Norwegian escort ships lay by and took no action, although shortly afterwards the Norwegian government lodged a bitter and vehement protest with the British over this violation of their territorial waters.

British, French and Polish soldiers on a hillside overlooking the Norwegian port of Harstad watch smoke rising from a fuel dump hit by Luftwaffe bombs. The Nazi blitz through Norway was so quick that invading Allied soldiers such as these often arrived at strategic objectives only to find they had been destroyed or seized by the Germans.

The Royal Navy's display of muscle aroused tremendous enthusiasm among the British public, but its chief effect was at the Führer's headquarters in Germany. The British violation of Norwegian waters seemed to confirm Quisling's warnings of an impending British occupation of the country. It also convinced Hitler that the Norwegians, despite their anguished protests to the British government, would not physically oppose Allied infringement upon their neutrality. Then and there Hitler put an urgent priority on the conquest of Norway—and added Denmark almost as an afterthought, since Danish airfields would provide additional protection for the Norwegian action and might be useful as bases for an operation against Britain.

Unlike Churchill, Hitler had no worries about committee approval. "Equip ships. Put units in readiness," he ordered his High Command, and instructed it to produce a plan for the immediate invasion of Norway. As worked out during the next few days, under Hitler's personal supervision, the plan they produced was a model of breathtaking scope and daring. With a force scarcely bigger than the one the Allies were at that very moment pasting together for their own invasion scheme, Hitler's staff proposed the simultaneous seizing of every major port and airfield in the whole thousand-mile length of Norway. The date agreed upon was April 9, one day after the Allies were scheduled to go ashore.

In order to get all their own troops onto the beach on the same day along the strung-out Norwegian coast, the German ships staggered their departure times from their home ports. Transports carrying troops and supplies sailed several days early; other ships got under way on the mornings of April 7 and 8. As in Poland, Führer weather prevailed—in this case fog and storms that concealed the shipping movements, though it made things uncomfortable for the soldiers packed in the holds. When, on the night of the 7th, a group of German ships was sighted by British air reconnaissance, the British Admiralty made the disastrous mistake of assuming that it was the German war fleet putting to sea to interfere with the British landings in Norway. Britain's expeditionary force had already been embarked on cruisers in the port of Rosyth in the Firth of Forth. They were abruptly put ashore, leaving all their equipment on board, and the cruisers went off to look for the German fleet.

All other available British warships, except for those already on their way to mine the entrance to the port of Narvik, were ordered out of the main naval centers of Rosyth, Scapa Flow and the Clyde to hunt down the Germans. The mine-laying operation was completed between 4:30 and 5:00 in the early morning of April 8, and the ships of the mining force were then withdrawn to join the main British fleet in the search; in the meantime the Germans' vulnerable transports and escorts slipped past them in the fog.

Late that day the Norwegian government in Oslo became aware that two mighty, contending powers were about to sweep down on their country. Next morning the authorities gave orders for partial mobilization, and sent out orders to the troops—by mail. The letters were barely in the Oslo post office when the first Germans arrived in Scandinavia.

An hour before dawn on April 9, the Germans landed at Oslo—and Copenhagen. Denmark, a small, flat country with only a minuscule peacetime army and totally unprepared for war, was conquered in four hours. A troopship loaded with German soldiers tied up, unchallenged, at the Copenhagen docks; a motorized brigade followed by two infantry divisions crossed the Danish-German land frontier and paratroopers dropped on the Aalborg airfield.

Amidst a scattering of shots, the invaders overwhelmed the Royal Guard and occupied the headquarters of the Danish Army, and a Luftwaffe demonstration over Copenhagen was the clincher. General Kurt Himer, chief of staff for the German task force, later wrote that the planes "roaring over the Danish capital did not fail to make their impression: the Government accepted the German requests" to submit to what the Germans called the "protection of the Reich." When the brief encounter was over, total casualties on both sides were 56 killed and wounded.

Almost simultaneously, German forces hit the Norwegians, who were more inclined to fight back. But the suddenness of the German onslaught completely undid them. Despite all the plotting by Quisling, treason played no major part in the Nazi takeover. German armed forces simply turned up by sea or air at all the main strategic points of the country, and while the Norwegians were still rubbing their eyes they found that they had been occupied.

However, they still managed to put up some semblance of a struggle. At the entrance to the Oslo Fjord the patrol-

GERMAN EXODUS FROM THE BALTIC STATES

A German woman (right) sits at a customs table piled with silver seized from her fellow deportees.

Ads in a German-language paper offer the household belongings of hurriedly evacuated Germans, including a writing desk, lamps, kitchenware, and a carpet—all put up for sale at a fraction of their original cost.

Crates and cartons and suitcases full of articles left behind by Germans fill an Estonian warehouse.

In the fall of 1939, the 120,000 Germans living in the Baltic countries of Estonia, Latvia and Lithuania seemed a risk to Joseph Stalin; fearing Hitler might use their presence as a pretext for a takeover, the Russian dictator ordered the Germans out.

Though he privately raged at Stalin's affront, Hitler reluctantly went along. He had just signed a nonaggression pact with the Soviets, and in 1939 was not yet prepared for war with the Soviets.

Evacuation orders issued on October 9 gave the Baltic Germans three weeks to leave. Many families had lived in the region for centuries and had accumulated great wealth and enormous estates—but they could take along only $23.50 in currency, $100 in gold and 110 pounds of luggage. Those trying to sneak valuables out were, for the most part, caught. Household goods were sold for disaster prices; many precious possessions were simply abandoned. On October 30, the last Germans filed aboard transports and sailed off under the watchful eye of the Russian Navy.

boat *Pol III*, a 214-ton guard boat with one gun, sighted a German flotilla slipping through the darkness toward Oslo. Captain Wielding Olsen attacked with his single gun and was shelled in return. Both his legs were shot off, but before he rolled overboard to die in the icy water he managed to ram and damage the torpedo boat *Albatros*.

German warships, led by the heavy cruiser *Blücher*, continued up the fjord toward the ancient fortress of Oscarsborg. As they reached it, the fort opened fire. Its armament dated back to the turn of the century, but it was still deadly. Eight- and 11-inch shells from the fortress' old guns ripped into the *Blücher* and set her ablaze; explosions racked the cruiser, and she went down with the loss of over a thousand men. Among them were Gestapo agents assigned to arrest the King and officers who were to have staffed German army headquarters in Oslo. The rest of the German ships withdrew hastily, though not for long.

In the respite provided by the defenders of Oscarsborg, 67-year-old King Haakon VII was whisked to the Oslo railroad station to board a waiting train and foil German plans to use him as a puppet. With him were the Crown Prince and Princess and their three small children. Most of the members of the government hurriedly joined the royal party, taking with them the Foreign Office archives and the bullion of the Bank of Norway—23 tons of it.

The train headed north for Hamar, the first stop on an odyssey that was to continue for many days as German bombs and bullets relentlessly pursued the fleeing King and his cabinet. At one of his brief stops Haakon, his face gaunt from lack of sleep and his clothes showing signs of wear and tear, said sadly, "All civilization seems to have come to an end. I cannot understand how such terrible things can happen." Eventually he reached Tromsö and on June 7 sailed aboard the cruiser *Devonshire* to Britain, where he formed a government-in-exile and banked the bullion.

For a short period after King Haakon and his family first took flight, there were no German troops in Oslo, and an effective defense might have been mounted if the military leadership had been alert. But the small Norwegian force stationed in and around Oslo had been thrown into confusion and failed to take full advantage of the brief breathing space —for example, no one thought to place any obstacles to landing aircraft on the runways of the Fornebu airfield; and when German planes came in with their loads of heavily armed infantry, the antiaircraft defenses did little more than slow their landing and inflict minor casualties. When these first arrivals disembarked, 120 Norwegian soldiers were killed or wounded resisting them.

The entire invading force, however, still amounted to only a few hundred fighting men and a military band, and could have been wiped out by a determined counterattack. But its temporary commander, a Luftwaffe attaché stationed in Oslo, was a man of nerve. Instead of worrying about hostile action, he snapped his men into formation behind the oompah-ing band and marched them brazenly down Oslo's boulevards, completely unopposed. The city of 250,000 people was taken over without another shot being fired.

In the course of the tragicomic day, Vidkun Quisling first proclaimed himself Prime Minister and next attempted to form a pro-German government. The first worked better than the second because almost all the Norwegian officials still in Oslo refused to serve under Quisling. When he went on the radio to announce himself as the new Norwegian ruler, his appeal for support fell on deaf ears, since the great majority of the Norwegian people wanted nothing to do with him or with his Nazi ideology. The police would not take orders from him, civil servants failed to show up for work, and Oslo workers threatened to go on strike.

For the Germans, however, the operation was proceeding smoothly. While the Royal Navy was still searching in the fog for the phantom grand fleet, German transports and their escorts pulled boldly into Norwegian seaports. The heavy cruiser *Hipper* and four destroyers ran at full speed past the shore batteries guarding Trondheim and pulled, unscathed, into the harbor. Though the garrisons in the outer harbor fought on until dusk, the city itself fell without resistance.

Down the coast at Bergen, shore guns crippled the cruiser *Königsberg* and an auxiliary ship, but other German ships took refuge behind anchored Norwegian ships and their troops landed unhurt. Further south, at Stavanger, a Norwegian destroyer sank the German munitions ship *Roda*, but could do nothing to prevent the occupation by paratroops of the big airport at nearby Sola. At Kristiansand, nearly 200 miles from Oslo, Norwegian shore batteries held off a German squadron for several hours before receiving a message

Britain's brand new Prime Minister, Winston Churchill, emerges from Number 10 Downing Street followed by his Parliamentary private secretary, Brendan Bracken. Churchill, who from 1932 on had vainly urged British preparedness—and a stronger line against Adolf Hitler—had been called to power on May 10, 1940, exactly five days before Holland would fall and as both Belgium and France were being threatened.

in their own code, which the Germans had broken: "British and French destroyers coming to your aid, do not fire." Following instructions, the guns fell silent, and ships carrying German assault troops steamed safely past them.

By day's end, the British had awakened to the dangerous German successes in Norway, and had started sending some real help. Royal Navy warships moved shoreward out of the fog and turned their guns on the German ships in the fjords and harbors with devastating effect. The submarine *Truant* torpedoed the cruiser *Karlsruhe* at Kristiansand, and RAF dive bombers finished off the damaged *Königsberg*. Next day, the British submarine *Spearfish* torpedoed and heavily damaged the pocket battleship *Lützow* near Oslo.

But for the moment, the active British role in the battle was all naval. British troops, originally assembled for the Narvik expedition, were still at Rosyth; it took precious time to get them back on board ship—and even more time to organize reinforcements now needed to cope with the Germans. The available backup troops were minimal: three French Alpine battalions, French Foreign Legionnaires and a Polish contingent. But even feverish haste could not get these arrangements completed before the main Norwegian airfields and ports had fallen into German hands. After that, there was no way that the Allies could land enough troops to prevent the conquest of the entire country.

Only in the far north did there seem to be a chance of saving something from the wreckage of the campaign. At Narvik, the terminus of the Road of Iron and the Allies' own original target, the German forces, hundreds of miles from their bases, were unsupported by aircraft and short of supplies. To Allied planners looking for a way to recoup, this force looked like the easiest target.

Indeed, one of the few things these Germans had going for them was a first-rate commander, General Eduard Dietl. From the moment they landed from a destroyer fleet on April 9, the situation had deteriorated. Early the following morning a British destroyer flotilla prowling Narvik harbor in a snowstorm had surprised the German squadron at anchor. By the time the action was over the British ships had sunk three German destroyers, damaged five others and blown up a munitions vessel.

Within three days, General Dietl's plight had become desperate. A British battleship, the *Warspite*, with nine destroyers, had entered the narrow waters of the fjord leading to Narvik and had wiped out the remaining German naval forces protecting Dietl's position. To hold Narvik, Dietl had 4,600 men; although almost half of them were picked mountain troops, the remainder were sailors with no infantry training who had fled sinking and damaged ships.

But once again, the Germans were decisive while the Allies fumbled. Long-range Luftwaffe planes made artillery drops, while the Swedes were persuaded by the Nazis to let medical supplies be ferried into Narvik over the Swedish railways. Meanwhile, the British were bogged down in contradictory orders and interservice wrangling. The naval force commander, Admiral of the Fleet the Earl of Cork and Orrery, wanted to launch an immediate attack. His orders, given him verbally by Churchill, had been to "turn the enemy out of Narvik at the earliest possible moment" and "to act with all promptitude in order to attain this result." Conversely, however, the written instructions from the War Office for General P. J. Mackesy, military commander of the ground forces that accompanied the naval squadron, were to "ensure the cooperation of the Norwegian forces" before taking any action, and carry out a landing only when he had sufficient troops. "It is not intended," said the orders, "that you should land in the face of opposition."

When Lord Cork urged General Mackesy—he could not order him—to attack Narvik without delay, the General pointed out that Dietl's machine-gun posts were in firm control of Narvik, and that the ground forces were prepared only for an unopposed landing, not for a direct assault on the town. Struggling through three feet of snow under German machine-gun fire, Mackesy argued, the troops would have little chance. A landing, said the General, would inevitably result in the "snow of Narvik being turned into another version of the mud of Passchendaele," a reference to the World War I battle that had cost the British a quarter of a million casualties.

Although the British War Office soon modified its orders to Mackesy, the General persisted in his cautious approach. After a series of timid advances aimed at gradual encirclement of the town, Mackesy finally gave his reluctant assent to a major landing on May 12. But the delay had given Dietl the opportunity to consolidate his position.

Not surprisingly, Mackesy was relieved the next day by

the more vigorous General C. J. E. Auchinleck. And on the 28th of May Narvik was finally taken by French and Norwegian troops. Dietl, however, was still holding on to 100 square miles of Norwegian territory in the mountains above Narvik when the Allies, faced by greater disasters closer to home, had to withdraw their troops from the area. Thus they left the entire country in German control.

From start to finish, the Norwegian campaign lasted less than two months at the relatively minor cost to the Germans of just under 5,000 casualties in missing, wounded and dead. They had surprised and humiliated their enemies by mounting a successful amphibious operation in the face of Allied navies that were many times more powerful than their own. The invading forces the Germans had launched had been, in the final count, no larger than the Allied contingent sent in pursuit of them. They were, however, much better handled; and where they lacked strength they made up for it with bluff and imagination.

All in all, the German foray into Scandinavia appeared to Hitler as a totally successful action, even more pleasing than the Polish operation, because in this case he did not have to share the spoils with the Russians.

There were some negative results for Germany, however. Admiral Raeder had lost more than half his navy, which had been sunk or crippled in the Norwegian fighting. Three cruisers, 10 destroyers, six U-boats, one gunnery training ship and 10 smaller vessels were destroyed, and five cruisers were seriously damaged. It may have seemed a small price to pay for the rich prize of Norway, but within a very short time the lack of those ships would prove to be one of the decisive factors in preventing Hitler from delivering a death blow to his enemies by invading England. Operation *Sea Lion,* the German plan for landing in Britain, had to be postponed from early summer to September and finally had to be abandoned in favor of an air assault.

In Britain, the Norwegian campaign had a political consequence that was resoundingly and positively decisive. By early May it was clear that the Allied effort in Norway was an abysmal failure. The traumas of defeat, the repeated examples of blundering and indecision in high quarters had brought the normally placid public of Great Britain to a boiling rage. Prime Minister Neville Chamberlain still had a com-

fortable majority in Parliament. However, even his most loyal supporters were beginning to doubt that he was the man to lead his country in a war—which, it was now obvious, was going to be much longer and harder than anyone had anticipated. Still, discipline was strong in the Prime Minister's Conservative Party, and Chamberlain continued in the insouciant confidence that he could survive Norway just as he had survived the successive disasters of Czechoslovakia, of Poland and of Finland.

In the Parliamentary session set for May 7, one of the speakers was an aging Conservative M.P., a genuine spokesman for the British Establishment: Leopold Amery, who had been a schoolmate of Churchill at Harrow a half century before. The house was packed and angry, ready for denunciations of Chamberlain's policies.

Amery began in the conventional jocular way. The British record in Norway reminded him, he said, of a young friend who had gone lion hunting in East Africa:

"He secured a sleeping car on the railway and had it detached from the train at a siding near where he expected to find a certain man-eating lion. He went to rest and dream of hunting lion in the morning. Unfortunately, the lion was out man-hunting that night. He clambered on to the rear of the car, scrabbled open the sliding door, and ate my friend. That is in brief the story of our initiative over Norway."

He then went on to give a pitiless analysis of the fearful shortcomings of the British government. In his peroration, Amery borrowed a line employed by Oliver Cromwell when he dissolved Parliament in 1653. Turning toward Neville Chamberlain, Amery said:

"You have sat too long here for any good you have been doing. Depart, I say, and let us have done with you. In the name of God, go!"

It was exactly what the British people had been saying in their hearts for a long time. Chamberlain was swept out of office, and Winston Churchill was called on to form a government of genuine national unity. Here at last they felt they had a leader capable of taking on Hitler, one who would never let go of his enemy's throat until that enemy had died. Churchill's accession to power came none too soon. For on the very day—May 10, 1940—that he presented his new government to Parliament, the long-delayed storm of the German assault broke on the Western Front.

THE WINTER WAR

BITTER HARVEST IN THE ARCTIC

A snow-masked sign in the village of Suvilahti locates Finnish towns near the Soviet border; the burning buildings have been hit by Russian bombs.

When the Soviet Army High Command attacked Finland in November of 1939, there seemed little reason to expect anything but a swift and complete victory. The hugely outnumbered Finns had no more than a few tanks and an air force of obsolete biplanes to put up against the latest mechanized units of the Soviet Army. And since the Russians believed they would crush Finland in 12 days at the most, they saw little reason to worry about Finland's arctic cold.

They were dead wrong. It took the Soviets more than half the winter, which turned out to be the coldest in a century, to subdue the tough, weather-wise Finns. Soviet tanks, stuck in deep-drifted snow and paralyzed by temperatures of 40 to 50 degrees below zero, were easily destroyed by artillery grenades and hand-thrown gasoline bombs. Thousands of Russian infantrymen, hurled into the attack without proper cold-weather clothing, were crippled by frostbite. Red soldiers learned that a man who touched the bare metal of his rifle with ungloved hands risked stripping off skin. Severely wounded men often froze to death in grotesque contortions, while others who might have been saved perished for want of blood plasma, which the weather turned to ice.

By contrast, the Finns were well prepared for the winter war. For the field, they wore warm, snow-camouflaged clothes, and in the fortifications of the Mannerheim Line, named for the Finnish commander-in-chief, they stayed firm and relatively snug in quarters that shielded them from both shells and cold, and that included such amenities as saunas.

Underground shelters protected Finnish civilians, as well against the Soviet air attacks that swept over from Russia whenever the weather was clear. But the most efficient shelters were in such cities as Helsinki and Viipuri; in rural areas the bombs fell on relatively unprotected villages and towns. Many country-dwelling civilians, their homes destroyed, were cast out onto snowy roads (page 97), or forced to take miserable refuge in forests (page 99). In March 1940, when the Russians finally overwhelmed the defenders with irresistible masses of men and steel, 400,000 Finns fled the territories of eastern Finland that were ceded to the Soviets

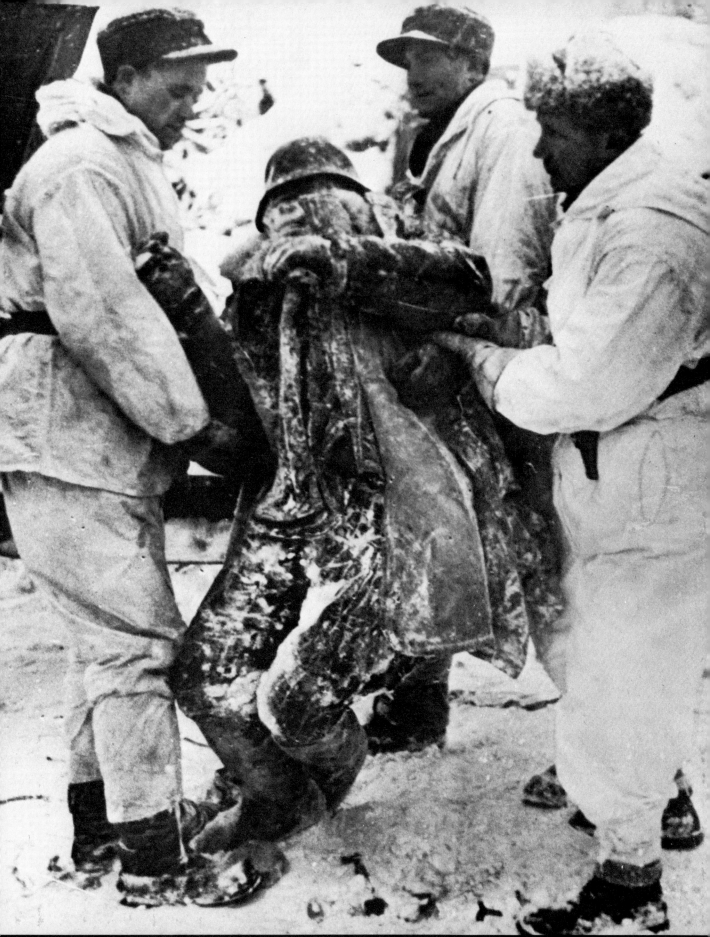

Finnish soldiers heft the rigid corpse of a Russian officer who fell from a gunshot wound and froze with one of his arms still raised in front of his face.

A Finnish soldier (above) guards the camouflaged entrance to a bunker on the Mannerheim Line, which was so well constructed that during one dawn-to-dusk shelling by the Russians no soldier inside was killed. At right, a well-fed, uniformed Finnish clerk in an underground command post catches a smoke while his comrades keep up with staff duties. Next to the inkwell in the foreground lie a pair of German-type potato masher hand grenades. On a rear wall, a Russian-language leaflet that had been air-dropped among Soviet troops exhorts the winter-weary Red Army soldiers to surrender to the Finns.

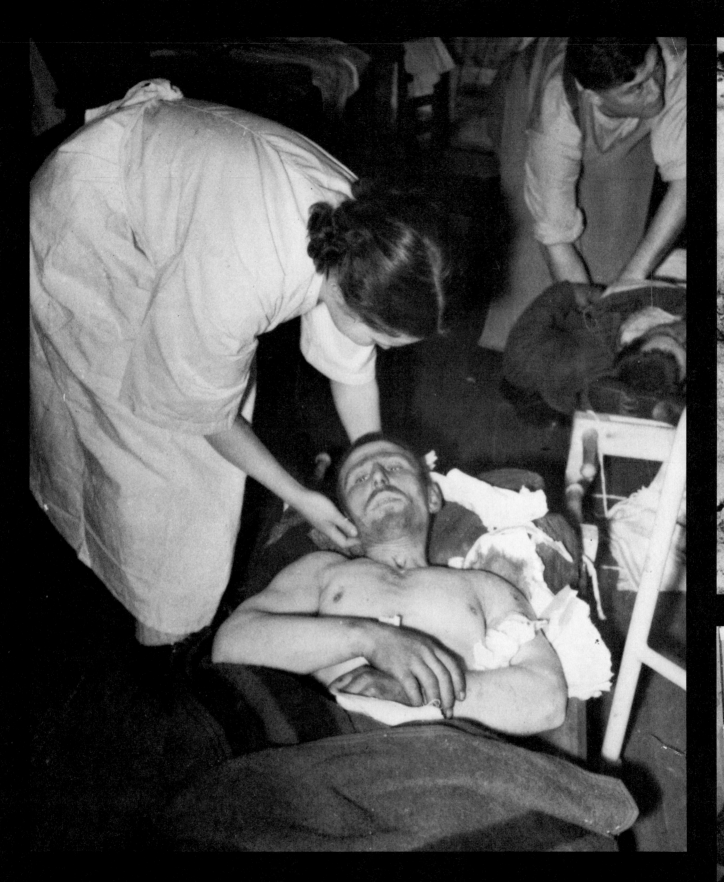

A wounded Russian, captured in a skirmish, is treated by a nurse in a Finnish field hospital. Russian soldiers were told by Red Army political officers that they would be shot or tortured by the Finns if they let themselves be captured. Despite this warning, many Russians surrendered to the Finns—and were alive and unharmed after the Soviet victory.

Subzero cold killed these Russian infantrymen as they sat immobile in their foxhole. Partly as a tactic of a fluid, evasive defense, partly to avoid freezing, Finnish soldiers were under orders to keep in constant motion when not sheltered in their heated underground bunkers.

Captured Red Army soldiers, in makeshift winter uniforms, display their frostbitten hands as they await aid in a Finnish hospital. In such cases, surgeons often had to amputate fingers and even entire hands.

Wounded Finnish soldiers rest on wooden stretchers in a cabin serving as a temporary front line first-aid station. Although the Finns suffered 70,000 casualties, they inflicted nearly 10 times as many on the Russians.

A Finnish home in the city of Viipuri burns after being struck by bombs during an air raid. The medieval city was a prime Russian aerial target because it commanded the all-weather highway leading from the Mannerheim Line to the Finnish capital at Helsinki.

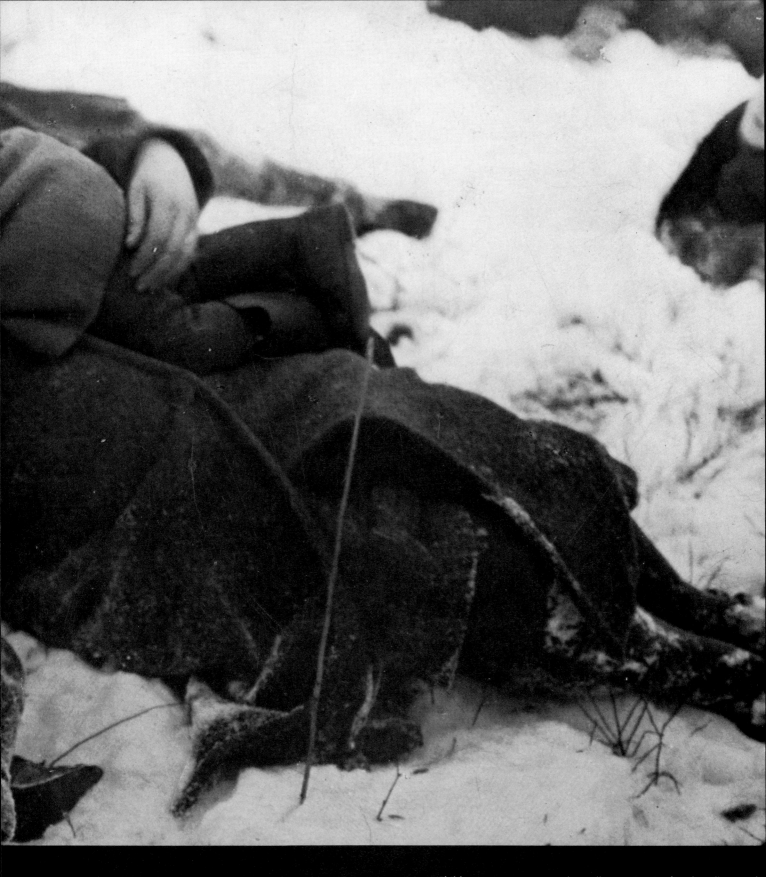

Children cower on a snowy forest floor as Russian bombers fly over the nearby town of Tammisaari. To protect themselves against the constant air raids, many noncombatants spent whole days camping out in the woods.

THE BRILLIANT EXILES

Anti-Nazi German author Thomas Mann and his wife, Katya, who left Germany in 1933, stand at the rail of the ship that brought them to the U.S. in 1939.

A DECADE'S DRAIN OF BRAIN AND TALENT

"Hitler is my best friend," declared Walter Cook, director of New York University's Institute of Fine Arts during the 1930s. "He shakes the tree and I collect the apples."

Cook, a passionate anti-Nazi, was referring with satisfaction to the host of talented people who fled Europe to escape Germany—and Fascist Italy and civil-war-torn Spain—finding refuge in the United States and employment in institutions like Cook's. Between 1930 and 1941, over 25,000 gifted artists, musicians, writers, scientists and scholars came to America; thousands more took refuge in Britain.

Of these emigrés, the great majority were Jews, whose lives, livelihood and property were in danger both from rightist regimes and the bullyboy street-fighters that Hitler and Mussolini encouraged. Others were Communists, Socialists and liberals of every stamp, who left to save both their lives and careers from the persecution meted out to ideological nonconformists. Still others decamped because they wanted to preserve artistic or intellectual standards that had been rejected or forbidden by Nazism and Fascism. Some migrated to build better careers in countries anxious to welcome them—or simply to work in surroundings not yet stained by terrorism and war.

The result was the incalculable loss to Europe—and gain to the United States and Britain—of such towering figures as theoretical physicist Albert Einstein, conductor Arturo Toscanini and novelist Thomas Mann. More precisely measurable in historical terms was the impact generated by the departure of a group of nuclear physicists that included Hans Bethe, James Franck and Enrico Fermi—men who helped to develop the atomic bomb.

Even when this migration of scientists was first starting, perceptive people in the totalitarian countries importuned against it—but Hitler, for one, did not listen. After hearing a 1933 protest from the eminent mathematician and physicist Max Planck at the firing of 1,600 teachers from German universities, the Führer replied: "If the dismissal of Jewish scientists means the annihilation of contemporary German science, we shall do without science for a few years."

Sigmund Freud, the Jewish founder of modern psychoanalysis, left Austria and fled to Britain via Paris with his daughter, Anna, in June 1938.

Impresario Max Reinhardt, on the Normandie in 1937 en route to New York, was already known in America for his film A Midsummer Night's Dream.

NOVELISTS AND PLAYWRIGHTS

◄ Novelist Erich Maria Remarque, *a German, came to New York September 4, 1939, on the liner Queen Mary; his country had attacked Poland while he was at sea. Remarque had been in bad odor with the Nazis since his successful 1929 novel, All Quiet on the Western Front—an exposé of front-line horrors of World War I. Hitler had had copies of the book publicly burned in front of Berlin University in 1933, claiming that it "displayed treachery toward the soldiers of the World War."*

Poet-dramatist Bertolt Brecht *was a Marxist whose egalitarianism brought him fame—and Hitler's antagonism. His villains were the industrialists of In the Jungle of Cities; his heroes were the little people of The Threepenny Opera. When Hitler became Chancellor in 1933, Brecht fled via Denmark and Sweden. His abandoned manuscripts were hidden by a friend, then shipped in trunks across Siberia to Brecht in southern California.*
▼

Novelist Lion Feuchtwanger *declared on a United States lecture tour in 1933 that there were "about 139,900 mistakes in 140,000 words" of Hitler's Mein Kampf. Hitler retaliated by confiscating Feuchtwanger's Berlin home. Resettled in France, he was arrested in 1939 by the French and imprisoned as an enemy alien. In the confusion following the fall of France in 1940 he escaped to America through Lisbon.*
▼

▲
Novelist Franz Werfel *was famed in the 1930s for his work, The Forty Days of Musa Dagh, and his play, Jacobowsky and the Colonel. Czech-born but long resident in Vienna, he was in Italy when the Nazis took over Austria in 1938. Werfel, a Jew, went to Paris and, when Germany invaded France in June 1940, escaped and for seven weeks hid in Lourdes. There he vowed if he got to America he would pay tribute to Lourdes' patron saint, Bernadette. Safe in New York by the fall of 1940, he wrote the best seller, The Song of Bernadette.*

Author André Maurois, *France's best-known ►
Jewish writer and an outspoken anti-Nazi, served as liaison officer with the BEF in France at the start of World War II—at one point posing for the press while aiming a British tank gun (right). After the fall of France the following June, Maurois went to Britain, this time as a private spokesman for his country. Jobless in Britain, and unable to return safely to German-occupied Paris, he flew from London late in 1940 to take a teaching post in Boston.*

◄ **Physicist Enrico Fermi,** married to a Jew, departed Italy in December 1938 after Mussolini, having received pressure from Hitler, passed laws depriving Jews of political and economic rights and opportunities. Stopping in Stockholm long enough to pick up a Nobel Prize for his pioneering analytical work on neutrons, Fermi arrived in the United States in January 1939. There in collaboration with other exiled nuclear physicists, including Hungarians Edward Teller and Leo Szilard, he worked on the development of the atomic bomb.

◄ **Mathematician Albert Einstein** was easily the most famous among Germany's refugee scientists. He was a 1921 Nobel Prize winner whose formulation of the Theory of Relativity and subsequent work in the forefront of theoretical physics had earned him worldwide recognition as a genius. Vilified by Hitler as a Jew, Einstein resigned from his directorship at Berlin's Kaiser Wilhelm Institute, renounced his German citizenship in 1933 and moved to the United States where he continued his work at Princeton's Institute for Advanced Study.

▲ **Political scientist Hannah Arendt** was a student at the University of Heidelberg when the Nazis were moving to power in the late '20s. Appalled by the sheeplike conformity of Hitler's followers and in danger because she was a Jew, she fled in 1933. In the U.S. in 1940, she taught at the New School for Social Research in New York and wrote widely on Nazi Germany.

▲ **Physicist Hans Bethe** came to the United States in 1935 and immediately got a teaching and research post at Cornell. He had been ousted as instructor at the German University of Tübingen, which he took philosophically: "Since I had a Jewish mother," he said, "it was clear to me that sooner or later I would have to leave. . . . I didn't expect it to be quite so soon." By 1943 his knowledge of thermonuclear energy made him part of the atomic project team. Until 1946 Bethe headed the theoretical physics division of the Los Alamos Science Laboratory—headquarters for atomic testing.

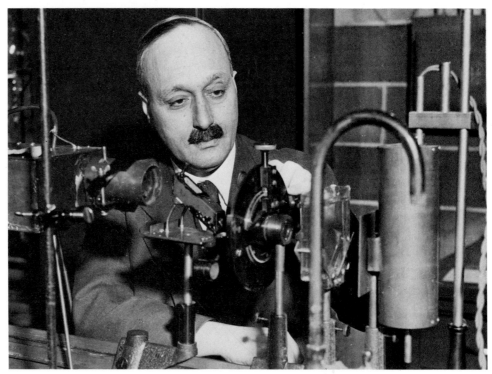

Physical chemist James Franck resigned his ► professorship at the University of Göttingen in 1933 in protest of Hitler's racist policies. Attacked by Nazis for "sabotaging the state," his value as a scientist was so great (he too was a Nobel Laureate) that, although he was Jewish, the German government offered to let him keep his job. Franck emigrated anyway; he moved to Copenhagen and, in 1935, to the United States, where he joined other European exiles in working on atomic projects.

◄ **Composer Kurt Weill** and his wife, Viennese singer-actress **Lotte Lenya,** were denounced by the Nazis in 1933 as "Kultur-Bolschewisten" —dangerously radical artists. Weill's principal crime was his association with Leftist writer Bertolt Brecht, for whom he wrote the score of The Threepenny Opera. Lenya was deemed equally guilty: she gained considerable fame in the role of Jenny in the same musical. The Nazis banned Weill's works and refused to let Lenya act.The couple shortly thereafter left Germany and within two years were in New York. There Lenya resumed her acting career and Weill set to work composing music for an epic Bible play by Franz Werfel, another emigré colleague.

Conductor Otto Klemperer came to the U.S. with his wife after he lost his job at the Berlin State Opera during the 1933 anti-Semitic purge. Though he promptly left Germany and became conductor of the Los Angeles Symphony, the Nazis still harassed him: they accused him—unjustly—of income tax evasion and confiscated all his German property.
▼

▲ **Composer Igor Stravinsky,** a Russian living in Paris in the 1930s, abhorred the cultural bias of the Nazis, who already had blacklisted the work of such other modern composers as Paul Hindemith. When he got an offer of a professorship at Harvard in 1939, Stravinsky —happy to put distance between himself and Hitler—departed for the United States in the summer of 1939, on the eve of war.

Conductor Arturo Toscanini claimed that the Italian Fascist hymn, "Giovinezza," was a musical absurdity, and refused to play it at concerts he conducted—a policy that earned him a beating by party toughs in Bologna in 1930. The experience intensified his hate of Mussolini, which he expressed loudly and frequently. But he loved Italy and refused to leave until, in 1938, the New York-based National Broadcasting Company tempted him with an orchestra created for him to conduct.
▼

Conductor Erich Leinsdorf was a youthful 26 in ► 1937, but for four years he had led the Salzburg Festival Orchestra as a protégé of Arturo Toscanini. Recommended by Toscanini to the manager of the Metropolitan Opera, Edward Johnson, Leinsdorf was hired, sight unseen, as an assistant conductor of the New York opera house. At that time, Hitler had not yet annexed Austria; but Nazi politics and musical taste were already limiting conductors' opportunities there as well as in Germany. Leinsdorf, realizing that his safety and economic future lay in America, joined the Met; in 1939, he became its Wagner specialist and chief conductor.

▲
Architects Walter Gropius (right) and **Marcel Breuer** founded a school called the Bauhaus, which had become a training ground for other modernists in the 1920s—and a powerful influence on design throughout Europe. By 1928, however, German antagonism to innovative art, spurred by the growing Nazi influence, impelled architect Gropius and furniture designer Breuer to resign from the Bauhaus. Both left Germany—Breuer to Spain, Switzerland and Britain and Gropius to London. Then, in 1937 they came to America together to teach at Harvard's School of Design.

Surrealist painter Salvador Dali was a maverick ▶ among Europe's premier artists of the 1930s. His chief goal in leaving his native Spain for France in 1929 appeared to be the avoidance of family conflict. Later, while many of his colleagues became passionately involved in the Spanish Civil War, Dali avowed utter disinterest. But he departed Europe when the Germans threatened Paris in 1940, and settled in the United States, where he occasionally retreated to the tranquillity of his bathtub.

Satirical artist **Saul Steinberg** emigrated to Milan from his native Rumania in the 1930s to study architecture and to draw. But the political atmosphere of Italy, which at one time had been congenial to free-thinking artists, became increasingly antagonistic. In mid-1940 Steinberg sailed for the Dominican Republic, and a year later made his entry into the United States.

▼

▲

Architect Ludwig Mies van der Rohe *became director of the Bauhaus after the first flight of its staff members in 1928, keeping it afloat for five more years despite increased hostility from the Nazis. In 1938, however, he at last gave up and left for the United States.*

Abstract artist **Josef Albers** *managed to keep out of political trouble from 1923 to 1933 despite efforts by the Nazis to suppress all avant-garde styles of art. By 1933, however, Albers' stubborn refusal to switch to the government-approved realism had earned such official animosity that he was forced to resign from his teaching position at the Bauhaus. Jobless, he came to the United States, where he became a member of the faculty of Black Mountain College, a North Carolina school that welcomed scores of exiled scholars and artists.*

▼

◄ **Caricaturist George Grosz** *attacked the Nazis with such ferocious socio-political satire that he was labeled Cultural Bolshevik Number One. Indeed, his mordant drawings of fat, middle-class Germans and smirking, bloodthirsty militarists could leave little doubt about where his sympathies lay. In the beginning, Grosz ignored Nazi pressures, which included anonymous threatening letters. But when a trusted assistant came to his Berlin studio in 1932 wearing a Storm Trooper's brown shirt and warned him to exercise more caution, Grosz decided to pack up. Fortunately, a position awaited him at New York's Art Students League, where he taught until he set up a school of his own in the same city.*

A March 1942 group show, entitled "Artists in Exile," at New York's Pierre Matisse Gallery brought together 14 European painters and sculptors who had found freedom and success in the United States. The exhibitors were, from left to right, first row: Matta Echaurren, Ossip Zadkine, Yves Tanguy, Max Ernst, Marc Chagall, Fernand Léger; second row: André Breton, Piet Mondrian, André Masson, Amédée Ozenfant, Jacques Lipschitz, Pavel Tchelitchew, Kurt Seligman and Eugene Berman.

113

4

After the harsh winter, it was one of the loveliest springs that anyone could remember. As evening fell pleasantly over Berlin on May 9, two friends met secretly and dined together for the last time. One was the Dutch military attaché, Colonel Jacob Sas; the other was Hans Oster, a high-ranking officer in the Abwehr, or German military intelligence service, and a staunch anti-Nazi.

For months, Oster had been funneling Hitler's war plans to his friend. *Fall Gelb (Case Yellow),* the German offensive against the Low Countries and France, was set to begin at 5 o'clock the next morning. Now Oster said: "The final order will be given at 9:30 [tonight]. If it is not countermanded between now and then, it will be definite."

When dinner was over, Colonel Sas accompanied Oster through the blacked-out streets to the headquarters of the German High Command and waited for him outside on the Bendlerstrasse. It was almost 10 o'clock when Oster came hurrying out. "There has been no cancellation," he said. "The invasion is to begin."

Colonel Sas sprinted back to his legation and put in a telephone call to the Ministry of War in The Hague. "I have only one thing to tell you," he said urgently. "Tomorrow at dawn. Hold firm. Have you understood me? Please repeat."

Within minutes of Colonel Sas's alert, Dutch political and military leaders were desperately preparing for the catastrophe. Orders flashed to their troops; defense plans swung into gear; emergency calls for assistance from the Allies whirred through the wires.

Precisely at dawn on the following morning, hundreds of German planes swept in over Allied air bases and communications centers in the north of France. Simultaneously a great, surging wave of tanks and infantry—the vanguard of an army of two million men—broke over the borders of Holland, Belgium and Luxembourg. The battle that was to decide the fate of the West had begun.

Aimed at Holland was the German Eighteenth Army, comprising an armored division, an airborne division carried in transports, a cavalry division, a motorized SS infantry division, six ordinary infantry divisions, and one picked infantry division of 12,000 men especially trained for air landings. In addition, two regiments of paratroopers, about 4,000 men, suddenly materialized over Holland and floated down from aircraft onto airfields and bridges. Four para-

FIRST BLOOD IN THE WEST

troop groups aimed for the big highway and railroad bridges at Moerdijk, Dordrecht and Rotterdam, and one other unit headed for the Dutch capital at The Hague.

The Dutch had assumed all along that they would be hit by armored forces on the frontier and by parachute troops dropped into their rear. They hoped to cut off and neutralize the latter before they could do fatal damage, and to slow down the former by slowly retreating, blowing up bridges and flooding the countryside as they went. If all went well, the attacking forces would be stalled on one side of a huge lake, while on the other—in "Fortress Holland," the populous stretch of coast between Rotterdam and Amsterdam—the defenders could settle down for a siege.

But before the Dutch could do more than destroy the bridges over the Ijssel River and some of those over the Maas River, the Germans were upon them. Parachute troops overpowered the Dutch bridge guards; wave after wave of air-transported units followed, landing alongside the bridges and even on the rivers in seaplanes. While the defenders were still trying to collect their wits, the Germans captured the bridges and held them against counterattacks as their armor came rumbling up from the frontier.

Part of the shock imparted by the German attack was generated by subterfuge. At the Gennep Bridge over the Maas, for example, three men in Dutch uniforms—two Dutch Nazis and one German—took the guard post by surprise and cleared the way for 11 more Dutch-uniformed men. This handful of impostors secured the bridge and held it while the German 265th Infantry crossed in an armored train, to unload 10 miles beyond the bridge and hit Dutch defenses elsewhere from the rear.

The largest group of airborne troops landed near The Hague. Their primary mission was to secure the airports for transport planes to land troops and prevent any Allied attempt to send airborne reinforcements to the Dutch. Next, several detachments were to dash into the city on motorcycles to round up the Dutch Queen and government officials, paralyzing the nation's resistance at its heart. Here the German plans went somewhat awry: the airfields were seized in the first phase of the assault, but the Dutch I Corps counterattacked and drove the invaders off the fields, rounding up 1,000 prisoners. The Hague, for the time being, was safe. But the main units of the German assault force withdrew to defensive positions in nearby villages, where they strenuously resisted efforts to pry them loose and tied down a disproportionate number of Dutch troops who were badly needed in other sectors.

Dark rumors and hints of treachery followed the parachute drops. It was said that some of the German prisoners were found to be carrying instructions for making contact with certain citizens of The Hague. This rumor gave rise to fears that the capital city was riddled with Fifth Columnists and Nazi sympathizers—traitors. As reports of parachutists began coming in from far and near, soldiers and civilians fell prey to ever wilder delusions: the parachutists were disguised as policemen, as traveling salesmen, as farm laborers, even as priests and nuns, and they were misdirecting traffic, poisoning wells, planting alarmist lies.

As a result of these tales, not only were troops who should have been at the front kept busy patrolling the rear and searching through cities and towns for largely nonexistent enemies, but also the notion that nearly anyone might be an enemy parachutist in disguise was often just the touch needed to turn the confusion caused by the real attack into full-scale chaos. (One paradoxical consequence, however, was that properly uniformed German parachutists were nearly lynched by Dutch housewives too outraged to fear them.)

Yet for all the crushing effectiveness of the attack and the accompanying confusion, Fortress Holland remained initially intact. Though German troops held the bridges leading to Rotterdam, Dutch defenders reacted swiftly to seal off the bridgeheads at the northern ends so that the enemy tanks could not cross them and deploy. There was still a chance, it seemed, that Allied reinforcements could arrive in time to help. The Dutch fought on, waited and hoped.

They might have waited forever. Allied plans to meet the expected attack on the Low Countries and France did not include provision for a major thrust in Holland; the Allies planned to meet the enemy in Belgium. As soon as the attack began, the French First Army was to advance through Belgium toward the rivers Dyle and Meuse. Units of the British Expeditionary Force under General Lord Gort would rush to protect Brussels while the Belgians defended Antwerp, Ghent and the Albert Canal. A small French force would keep an eye on the Ardennes; the bulk of the French forces

—43 divisions—would maintain fixed positions on the heavily fortified Maginot Line. Only the French Seventh Army, commanded by General Henri Giraud, was to advance to the region of Breda in southern Holland, where it could join up with the Dutch forces and close the gap between Antwerp and the Channel.

But the execution of these plans began too late for the Low Countries to cope with all the disasters that were descending. The Nazis pounced on Belgium. Royal Air Force and French Air Corps planes took wing to harass the oncoming enemy but scarcely dented their columns. Giraud's French Seventh Army, racing along the Channel to reach the Moerdijk bridges across the Maas estuary in Holland, which were held by German parachutists and airborne troops, was driven back by a combination of tank and Stuka attacks. The German 9th Panzer Division crossed the bridges at Moerdijk and Dordrecht and arrived at the southern approaches of the bridges to Rotterdam. On May 13, as Dutch defenses crumbled, Queen Wilhelmina and the government fled The Hague for London on a pair of British destroyers.

Only at Rotterdam did the German onslaught stall. Panzers were unable to break through the Dutch bridgeheads even though German airborne troops held the bridges leading to the city. Hitler lost patience. Demanding that "this resistance be broken *speedily*," he ordered the Luftwaffe to bomb the city into submission.

A massive air attack hit Rotterdam on May 14. Load after load of 2,200-pound delayed-action bombs rained into the heart of the city. In an area covering 642 acres, only a few buildings escaped total destruction. Among them were the town hall, stock exchange and post office. A margarine factory took a direct hit and spewed burning fat over blocks of the old town. Fires spread the destruction; thousands of the city's occupants were wounded in the avalanche of debris; more than 800 died. Some 25,000 houses were completely gutted, leaving nearly 78,000 civilians homeless.

The defenders of Rotterdam were thus bludgeoned into immediate capitulation. Late that evening the Commander-in-Chief of the Dutch forces, still holding The Hague, ordered a general cease-fire. In the five days of fighting, 2,100 Dutch troops had been killed and 2,700 wounded.

The bombing of the Netherlands' second largest city produced a highly unwelcome consequence for Hitler: the next day, British bombers that were based in France began hitting back at the important industrial cities in Germany's Ruhr Valley. But the attack on Rotterdam paid him an unexpected dividend as well. A wave of panic spread over the Western world. It was reported and believed that the Luftwaffe's merciless blasting of Rotterdam had killed 35,000 people and had destroyed the entire city. During the coming campaign in Belgium and France, thousands of civilians, fearing another Rotterdam, would clog the roads, seriously interfering with Allied military movements.

The wide, level gateway into Belgium through which the Germans had smashed their way in 1914 was guarded in 1940 by a series of ultramodern fortresses. The most formidable was Fort Eben Emael, north of Liège near the junction of the Albert Canal and the Meuse. Its 1,500-man garrison, alerted on the night of May 9, waited for dawn, secure in the knowledge that they were protected by thousands of tons of earth and concrete. They checked their equipment: electrically operated artillery—two 120mm guns and sixteen 75mm guns—secreted in well-camouflaged, well-armored apertures and sited to pour devastating fire on enemies coming from any direction.

Any direction, that is, except the air. At 4:30 a.m. on the 10th of May, 42 Junkers transport planes, each hauling a glider carrying a team of airborne troops that was trained in the use of special assault equipment, took off from Cologne for Fort Eben Emael and the Albert Canal bridges. At five minutes before dawn and the start of the main offensive, the 42 silent craft came skimming down on the gateway to the Belgian plain—which the Allies were convinced could be held for days, perhaps weeks.

One group of nine gliders swooped directly onto the roof of Eben Emael. A force of only 80 men, led by a sergeant, leaped out to storm the massive fort. In a maneuver rehearsed repeatedly in the preceding months, they set about cramming explosive charges into gunslits and ventilators and any other openings they could find. For the armored gun turrets they used a special hollow-charge demolition device —a brilliant technical innovation suggested by Hitler himself —that blew holes in steel and concrete and spewed flames into the interior, killing gun crews, smashing guns and filling the underground galleries with choking fumes.

HITLER'S STRATEGY FOR SEIZING WESTERN EUROPE

Legend:
- ⨪⨪⨪ MAGINOT LINE
- ⋀⋀⋀ SIEGFRIED LINE
- ⣿ ARDENNES FOREST
- ⋯⋯ DYLE LINE
- ⋯⋯ FRONT ON MAY 24
- ⋯⋯ DUNKIRK DEFENSE PERIMETER

Holland
Amsterdam
The Hague
Rotterdam
England
London
ARMY GROUP B
Germany
Ostend
Dunkirk
Nieuport
Ghent
Antwerp
Albert Canal
Calais
Belgium
Maastricht
Cologne
Boulogne
Lille
Liège
Fort Eben Emael
Namur
Rhine River
ARMY GROUP A
Noyelles
Arras
Dinant
Abbeville
Somme River
Dieppe
Amiens
Sedan
Meuse River
ARMY GROUP C
St. Valéry-en-Caux
Luxembourg
Saarbrücken
Seine River
France
Paris

Hitler's bold design for conquering Western Europe relied on speed, surprise, deception—and power. Arrayed along a 200-mile front facing Holland and Belgium, 30 Wehrmacht divisions (Army Group B) were scheduled to swoop through the Low Countries in a four-pronged attack.

Hitler hoped the Allies would regard that as the major threat and rush the best and readiest French and British troops north to help the Dutch and the Belgians hold their key defenses along Belgium's Dyle River.

The real thrust would come farther south through the Forest of Ardennes. Army Group A, whose 45 divisions included most of the Germans' armor and motorized infantry, would knife through a gap between the Maginot and the Dyle lines, race across France to the Channel, and then swing north to help Group B encircle and annihilate the nearly one million Allied troops Hitler hoped to entrap.

The Germans could then devour the rest of France at leisure—including the Maginot Line, whose enormous garrison was meant to be kept occupied by feints made by the 19 divisions of Army Group C.

From the start on May 10, 1940, both Germans and Allies enacted Hitler's scenario to perfection. At the first sign of attack Allied troops sped north to take on Army Group B, which nevertheless overran Holland in five days. In Belgium, other German units of

Group B pushed back Allied forces after swiftly reducing Belgium's vaunted strong point, Fort Eben Emael.

With the Allies committed and the Maginot garrison pinned down, Group A panzers smashed through the Ardennes Forest and raced to the French coast in 10 days.

After turning north, Army Group A joined Army Group B to drive the cornered Allies into a pocket around Lille by May 24. The whole left flank of this salient dissolved four days later when its battered Belgian defenders surrendered on orders from King Léopold, and by May 30, the surviving Allied troops had withdrawn behind a seven-mile-wide, last-ditch perimeter around the port of Dunkirk.

Flame throwers, discharged into the gunports, added to the fires that had already been started inside and thickened the acrid smoke. Within an hour after dawn, Eben Emael was a blinded giant, incapable of holding up the sweep of the invading armies. The garrison somehow managed to fight on; but at noon on May 11, surrounded by ground troops and pounded by Stuka attacks, the defenders of Fort Eben Emael laid down their arms.

The main force of the gliders had meanwhile landed on the west bank of the Albert Canal. Some 300 assault troops swarmed onto the three main bridges. Belgian defenders managed to blow up one bridge, but the airborne invaders took the two others intact. While the Germans clung to this toehold, transport planes dropped reinforcements by parachute. There were only 500 men in the drop, for most of the Reich's paratroopers were engaged in the assault on Holland. To make this small force look larger, General Kurt Student, Germany's paratroop commander, had conceived the idea of dropping dummy parachutists with explosive charges attached. These blew up with dramatic effect and helped to create confusion while the Stukas and panzers of General Fedor von Bock's Army Group B swept behind the assault troops onto the Belgian plain.

To meet this expected thrust, the Allied units in northern France began their advance to form a continuous front with the Belgian army along the Dyle and Meuse rivers. Everything went smoothly at first. Right on schedule, 22 French and British divisions marched up to take their place beside 15 Belgian divisions in front of Brussels and Antwerp. In the towns through which they passed, Belgian civilians cheered and threw flowers. And in their opening skirmishes with Bock's forces in northern Belgium, Allied troops had little difficulty in holding their ground.

But some officers were both concerned and suspicious. Was it possible that the Allied troops were walking into a Nazi setup? Adolf Hitler, watching the northward movement of the Allied armies, had the answer. As he later told associates, his gamble had paid off. "When the news came through that the enemy was moving forward along the whole front, I could have wept for joy; they had fallen into

A German motor column churns through a field in Holland, passing to one side of a roadblock of dynamited trees. Overwhelmed by the suddenness of the German strike, the Dutch abandoned carefully laid defense plans but still made attempts to slow the panzers with makeshift barricades—which included old trucks and buses dumped across their highways.

the trap. It was vital that they believe we were sticking to the . . . old plan, and they *had* believed it!"

Indeed, the Allies were completely unaware that a German deathblow was gathering momentum through the Ardennes in southern Belgium—the air-armor-infantry drive suggested to Hitler by General Erich von Manstein and assigned to General Gerd von Rundstedt's Army Group A.

To be sure, the French surmised that action of some sort could be expected in this sector. But, they reasoned, it would take the Germans a good nine or 10 days to get through the wooded ravines of the Ardennes—if they could get through at all—and to be in a position to cross the Meuse River. The Meuse, in turn, could easily be defended, and there would be plenty of time to bring up reinforcements if needed. On these assumptions, the French sent only light motorized forces to back up the Belgian defenders in the Ardennes, while they held the line along the Meuse with their Second and Ninth armies, consisting largely of second-class units, more poorly trained and equipped than those sweeping into Belgium farther north.

The first German armored units to penetrate the Ardennes negotiated the minefields near the Belgian-German border during the night of May 9, and easily pushed the French and Belgian defense back. By May 12, three armored divisions were on the Meuse between Dinant and Sedan.

The Meuse is a swift, narrow stream at that point, running between steep banks overlooked by hills on the French side of the Franco-Belgian border. The river line was an ideal defensive barrier, and the French had constructed dugouts on the bank, and hundreds of artillery posts on the heights above. Though the Germans had been training intensively for two months for just this operation and knew the location of every French gun almost to the inch, the position still seemed formidable.

So it might have been—without the support of German air power. For hour after hour from early morning on May 13, flying almost uninterruptedly in small groups, Stukas and low-level bombers came screaming over the Meuse, giving the defenders no rest. By 4 p.m., the French guns covering the river had been pounded into silence. The Germans briskly began crossing the stream in assault boats and inflatable dinghies, setting up pontoon bridges, and then establishing beachheads on the west bank.

When General Heinz Guderian, who was leading the attack, crossed the Meuse in an assault boat, he found the work of his waterborne troops proceeding in an atmosphere of almost carefree enthusiasm. "On the far bank of the river," he later wrote, "I found the efficient and brave commander of the 1st Rifle Regiment, Lieutenant Colonel Balck, with his staff. He hailed me with the cheerful cry: 'Pleasure-boating on the Meuse is forbidden!' I had in fact coined the phrase myself during the training we had had for this operation, since the attitude of some of the younger officers had struck me as too light-hearted. I now realised that they had judged the situation correctly."

German tanks now rumbled over the pontoons and immediately began cutting up the French army. The French counterattacks were desperate but late and badly coordinated; though some river-bank heights changed hands three or four times, the Germans were in control of the situation from the start. The French flung a mass of armor against the expanding German bridgeheads, but French tanks were slower than the Germans', their fuel range was shorter, and they lacked radio communication. More than 50 of them were destroyed by the panzers in a couple of hours. When the Allied air forces hit the German positions, they suffered crippling losses against a huge concentration of antiaircraft guns. By May 14, the RAF had lost 268 of the 474 aircraft it had been able to spare for France.

Once across the river in force, the German armor fanned out as it sliced westward and spread terror in the rear of the French forces. General Erwin Rommel, who had taken his 7th Panzer Division across the Meuse downstream from Guderian's corps, described the disruption: "Civilians and French troops, their faces distorted with terror, lay huddled in the ditches, alongside hedges and in every hollow beside the road. . . . Always the same picture, troops and civilians in wild flight down both sides of the road . . . a chaos of guns, tanks and military vehicles of all kinds, inextricably entangled with horse-drawn refugee-carts."

Colonel Charles de Gaulle, leading the 4th Armored Division to strike the southern side of Guderian's rapidly growing bulge, ran into a sight for which nothing in his life as a proud career officer had prepared him: droves of French troops shuffling southward, disarmed and dispirited. They had been overrun by the panzers and the Germans had shouted to them contemptuously from their tanks: "Drop your rifles and get the hell out of here—we don't have time to take you prisoner."

Twice de Gaulle attempted counterattacks against Guderian; twice he failed. A few of the French tanks, according to Guderian, "succeeded in penetrating within a mile of my advance headquarters in Holnon Wood. The headquarters had only some 20mm antiaircraft guns for protection, and I passed a few uncomfortable hours until at last the threatening visitors moved off."

By May 16, the French defense line was breached with a gaping hole that was 60 miles wide. Through this gap the tanks and armored cars and motorcycles came racing, just as de Gaulle had envisioned it in 1933 when outlining his own concept of the use of tanks in future wars: "They will open the road of great victories . . . their swift and profound effects will cause the enemy to collapse, as sometimes the breaking of a pillar can bring down a cathedral."

The success was so sudden and so great that the Germans found it hard to believe. Back at headquarters, their maps showed them a long and vulnerable-looking wedge being pushed into the French lines. But the staff could not grasp, as the men in the front lines could, the extent of the French Army's disarray; headquarters grew afraid that the tanks might go too far too fast, and get trapped.

Twice within the first few days after his breakthrough, Guderian found his advance being held up by cautious superiors, who wanted to give the infantry enough time to catch up with the tanks and to form a continuous, combined front, as they had done in World War I. Guderian knew that this was not World War I any more, that his best chance was to let the tanks run loose. He bullied and bluffed his superiors into amending their orders to let him "consolidate the bridgehead," and then interpreted this freely to mean that he could go where he liked.

But even Guderian had a moment of hesitation. On the first day of his breakthrough, he went up to visit one of his divisions and asked its commander whether he thought it best to send the whole division straight on west or to divert some units to the southern flank to protect it from possible counterattacks. One of the division's majors broke in with one of Guderian's own favorite phrases, *Klötzen, nicht Kleckern,* roughly, "Slug 'em, don't scatter 'em." Guderian wrote later: "That really answered my question." And to consolidate his independence, he took the precaution of stringing miles of telephone wire from his command post to his forward units so he could order them into attack without sending radio messages that could be intercepted by nervous commanders at higher headquarters.

Hitler was more nervous than anyone. He raved to General Halder that his commanders were throwing the battle away by sending the tanks too far forward without support on their flanks. It was only after many weary hours that Halder, a recent convert to the *Klötzen* principle, succeeded in calming the Führer down.

As the tanks swept forward, the entire German High Command got behind the aggressive urge to exploit what it now realized was the chance of a lifetime. Every tank, almost everything on wheels the Germans possessed, was packed into the bulge. Though it was widening and deepening with every hour, only prodigies of organization could avoid locking the 71 German divisions, 10 of them armored, into a permanent traffic jam. Day by day, the tanks raced on, with tens of thousands of refugees trailing down the roads away from them. "They fled," said one observer, "accelerating their cars, pushing their handcarts. . . . In their scattered houses, they had enjoyed relative safety. They preferred to congregate in long columns exposed to the enemy's fire. Their flight was suicide."

By May 20, Guderian's forward units were in Amiens and Abbeville; they had gone farther in 10 days than the Kaiser's World War I armies had been able to get in four years. That night German armor reached the sea at the little French village of Noyelles. The news was flashed to Hitler and he was "beside himself with joy," as his chief of staff, General Alfred Jodl, noted in his diary.

Hitler had good reason to rejoice. His calculated risk had produced one of those decisive events that change the course of wars and empires. At one stroke, Germany had wiped out the whole Allied plan for waging the war, split the opposing armies, and menaced half the Allied force with encirclement and annihilation. There were almost a million men who were rapidly becoming cut off in the north by the rush of the panzers to the sea, including the entire Belgian

THE WORKHORSE OF THE WEHRMACHT'S STABLE

The fast, maneuverable, formidably armed medium tank shown here was the cutting edge of the German sword that sliced through the Low Countries and France in May of 1940. With its 75mm gun, the Panzer IV could easily stand off and destroy the more lightly armed of Allied tanks. Against the better Allied tanks, such as the French Char B—which also carried a 75mm gun—and the more heavily armored but slower British Matilda, the Panzer IV's speed was a distinct advantage.

The Panzer IV, with its large fuel tank, could go 125 miles without filling up. The crew arrangements were also better than those of its rivals. The driver and a radio operator, who doubled as a machine-gunner, sat in the hull up front. The turret housed the commander, the gunner for the 75, and a loader. In contrast, the French Char B had an overworked crew of three; a driver and a machine-gunner in the hull; the commander, alone in the turret, had to load and fire the main gun.

Ironically, however, the Germans almost squandered the advantage the Panzer IV gave them by building only 278 of the tanks for the Western campaign. This shortsighted policy, born

of overconfidence, forced tank commanders to use the versatile vehicles sparingly. The record for applying this stinginess probably belongs to General Erwin Rommel, a brilliant tactician who was to become Germany's greatest tankman. When one of his columns was stalled in a village by a detachment of heavier French tanks, he ordered just one Panzer IV to attack the French rear. Firing point blank at a furious rate, the Panzer knocked out 14 of the French machines, which were too ponderous to maneuver in the narrow village streets.

Not even Rommel could make the Panzer IVs invincible, however. When caught by surprise—as they were near Arras when British and French armor fell on the flank of Rommel's advancing column—they showed a streak of vulnerability. French shells that were fired from close range penetrated the Panzers' armor, knocking out three of them. Soon after, the Germans modified the Panzer IV, giving it thicker armor and a more powerful gun. Thus improved, it became the workhorse German tank, better than a match for most Allied armored fighting vehicles throughout the War.

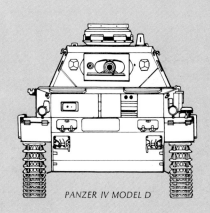

PANZER IV MODEL D

Weight: 20 tons
Length: 19 feet
Width: 9 feet
Height: 8 feet
Maximum speed on roads: 25 mph
Maximum speed cross country: 12 mph
Maximum range on roads: 125 miles
Maximum range cross country:
   80 miles
Fuel supply: 120 gallons
Trench-crossing capacity: 7 feet
Gradient-climbing capacity: 30°
Fording depth: 3 feet
Crew: 5
Armament: one 75mm gun,
   two 7.92mm machine guns
Front armor thickness: 1.2 inch
Side and rear armors: .8 inch
Roof armor: .4 inch

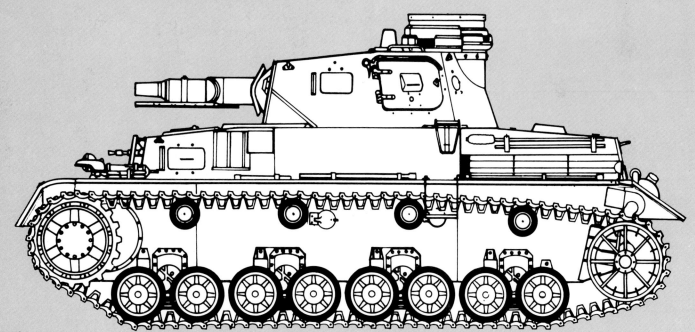

The original Panzer IV hull, designed in 1934, was used for all subsequent models, allowing mass production of more than 8,000 of these tanks.

Army, all but one of the divisions of the British Expeditionary Force and the two best of the French armies. Instead of fighting on terms of more or less equality with Bock's armies in Belgium, they now found themselves both hammered by Bock in front and threatened in their flank and rear by the scythe cut of Rundstedt's tanks.

Unless this combined Allied force could manage to break out quickly and to link up with the rest of the French armies south of the Somme, they would be hopelessly boxed up in northern France and western Belgium. Thus cut off, they could be supplied only through the Channel ports—Ostend and Niuewport in Belgium, and Boulogne, Calais and Dunkirk in France—and if worst came to worst, it was only through these ports that they could hope to escape.

By May 15, the worst was fast approaching for the Allies. At 7:30 a.m. that day, Prime Minister Winston Churchill was awakened by a telephone call from French Premier Paul Reynaud, who spoke as if under considerable stress. "We have been defeated," Reynaud said abruptly. "We are beaten; we have lost the battle."

The next day the stunned Churchill flew to Paris; "The situation," he found, "was incomparably worse than we had imagined." The sky over the Quai d'Orsay was wreathed with the smoke of official documents being burned outside government offices. As a witness commented, "Projected pacts, dreamed-of partitions and secret engagements thus returned to their natural element: smoke." But the super-careful bureaucrats had put copies of all these documents on a train sent—too late, as it turned out—to the south of France: the Germans intercepted the train and captured every scrap of paper anyway.

Meeting in Paris with Reynaud, Daladier and General Gamelin at the Quai d'Orsay, Churchill learned firsthand the grim details of the German breakthrough and the overwhelming rush of armor to the Channel coast. Turning to Gamelin, he asked: "Where is the strategic reserve?"—inquiring about the force that every general keeps ready to throw into a crisis. Gamelin shrugged his shoulders despairingly and replied that unfortunately there was none. In fact, Gamelin still had considerable reserves, but instead of the men being organized into a strong and ready counteroffensive force, they were scattered loosely all along the front.

Conceivably General Gamelin, if he had moved with dispatch and decision, could have done something to improve the situation. As a young officer in the desperate days of September 1914 he had helped in drawing up the plans that had stopped the Germans at the Marne. Now at 68 he must have been dreaming of doing the same thing, but he acted with a fatal lethargy. For nine days, from the start of the German offensive, he apparently did nothing himself. He left the running of the battle to his subordinate, General Alphonse Georges, although Georges was a man who was in poor health and one whom he had never trusted. On May 19 Gamelin went to Georges' headquarters, and found him in a state of "profound physical and moral depression." The senior general noted only a pretense of activity—a cacophony of jangling telephones and clacking typewriters, weary officers dispiritedly pushing around maps and files, and over all a stifling odor of stopped toilets.

Gamelin decided it was time to take over. He secluded himself and drew up a plan in which the Allied troops that were cut off in the north could break their way through the German corridor and French troops in the south could strike north to help them. Properly combined and executed, these actions might have cut off the tank spearheads and given the Allies a chance to form a new front along the Somme and the Aisne rivers.

Whether Gamelin's scheme could ever have been carried out is problematical. A simultaneous attack from north and south on the German corridor would have been a complex operation, even assuming the troops were rested and in fighting trim. In fact, at that moment most of them were either fighting for their lives or in flight under constant air attack; confused and exhausted, they were running out of ammunition. Gamelin could not even be sure where they were—in this war of movement, orders given one day might be hopelessly out of date the next because the front might have moved 20 miles overnight.

As it turned out, Gamelin's ruminations came to nothing. Paul Reynaud had had enough of this courtly, ineffectual generalissimo; the Premier replaced him with General Maxime Weygand, another hero of World War I, who was expected to be a symbol of dogged resistance. But France needed more than symbols. Weygand was 73; though his mind and his step were still lively, he was hardly the man for the hour. Arriving at his new command on the evening of May 19, he discarded the Gamelin plan and plunged into conferences with the Allied commanders in Belgium. Then, after three days, he drew up a plan that was almost indistinguishable from Gamelin's.

By this time, schemes for Allied offensives belonged more to the world of dreams than to the realm of practicality. The Allied armies were reeling, and the generals were in a state of shock. A British liaison officer described a meeting with General René Billotte, who was in command of all the French, British and Belgian forces in the north—those that were now principally threatened with destruction by the onrushing German thrust to the sea. Billotte spread out a map and began counting the red circles marking the location of the German armored divisions: "One panzer, two panzers, three panzers," he counted—all the way up to eight panzers. "And against them all I can do nothing," he kept repeating in a monotone. "I am dead tired, I am dead tired. And against them all I can do nothing."

General Billotte was killed in an automobile accident on the 21st of May, and was replaced by General Jean-Georges Maurice Blanchard, who had been commander of the French First Army. The change in command caused further delays and more confusion—and every passing hour of inaction brought the Allied armies closer to disaster. Arras, the original headquarters of the British Expeditionary Force, remained in Allied hands, but German forces, spearheaded by General Rommel's 7th Panzer Division, were fast approaching. A joint Franco-British drive was mounted to reinforce Arras and pinch off the German thrust. The BEF under Gort was still almost intact, and he threw two divisions and 74 tanks into the counterattack. Sixty tanks from the French 3rd Light Mechanized Division lent support. There was supposed to be a parallel French attack farther east; because of bad communications, it never was launched.

An attack could hardly have been set in motion under worse auspices. The German forces were much stronger than the Allies'; the German radio system was infinitely superior; Allied messages were intercepted. Yet, somehow or other, the Franco-British tank attack took the Germans by surprise, threw a crack SS motorized division into staggering disorder, and put a bad scare into Rommel, who reported that he was being attacked by hundreds of tanks.

Although the blow shocked the German High Command, it did not faze them for long. Rommel drove back the Allied onslaught with artillery and antitank guns, then brought up his tanks to smash it. The Allies were stopped with a loss of more than 40 of their tanks; the Germans lost scarcely more than a dozen. This fighting near Arras continued for several days, but the main German advance continued unchecked. No wonder, then, that General Blanchard, already weary when he replaced Billotte, now succumbed to the epidemic paralysis of will. Marc Bloch, the distinguished French historian who was a headquarters officer under Blanchard, described him "in tragic immobility, saying nothing, doing nothing, but just gazing at the map spread on the table, as though hoping to find on it the decision that he was incapable of taking."

"From the beginning to the end," observed Bloch, "the metronome at headquarters was always set at too slow a beat." Though Weygand was now convinced that the war was lost, he continued to put out absurdly optimistic communiqués, and misinformed his own generals about the increasingly catastrophic situation. He was still talking about stopping the German drive to the sea two days after the Germans had reached the coast. On May 26, when everything was coming apart in the north, he telegraphed Gort and Blanchard that they should attack southward "with confidence and the energy of a tiger," and assured them that a French advance from the south was "in very good shape." It was in no shape at all; there could be no attack of any significance in the south.

The battle in the Low Countries was finished. On the 28th of May, after 18 shattering days of seeing his small, tough forces torn to shreds, Léopold of Belgium—acting not as King but as Commander-in-Chief of the Belgian armed forces—capitulated to the Germans. Stukas were already roaming, unchecked, over the length and breadth of France, covering the unimpeded drive of the panzer divisions. Indeed, there was no force that was capable of effectively slowing the advance of the German tanks within the borders of continental France. As a result of this clear inexorability, by the time the first week of the Battle of France was over, influential voices in Paris were first whispering and then uttering aloud a word that only a few days before would have been branded as treasonous: Surrender.

PASSAGE OF THE PANZERS

A Dutch schoolboy in shorts and knee socks stares at a German tank commander who has halted to ask some infantrymen for directions on the way to the front.

IN THE BACKWASH OF THE BLITZKRIEG

The German attack that crushed the Low Countries in 1940 struck the Dutch and Belgians like an automobile accident: it was too rapid and catastrophic to seem real.

The assault that began on May 10 was over in Holland by May 15 and in Belgium on May 28. Even while it was underway, the lightning war had a surreal quality. A phalanx of steel tanks swept through. But after they had passed, terrible harbingers of conquest, the inhabitants could see windmills turning serenely in the fresh spring breeze; and the sun of the finest May in years shone down on blooming wildflowers and crops of barley ripening in the fields. Perhaps most incongruous of all to a populace weaned on tales of rapacious Huns was the initial conduct of the follow-up wave of German infantry, which was, according to at least one eye witness, "correct and surprisingly polite" toward civilians.

Yet in the quiet aftermath of the stunning armored conquest, the countryside was spotted with evidence of swift defeat. Long lines of enemy troops marched through quiet lanes, and their supply trucks churned up the dust of canal-side roads. Fires from bombs burned in the cities of Rotterdam, Brussels, Nivelles and Tournai. Streets were blocked by futile barricades thrown up in haste by retreating Dutch and Belgian forces, who also dynamited bridges and sank boats in canals in a vain effort to slow the German advance.

Working their way around these obstacles, processions of refugees wound southward across the landscape in cars, bicycles, on foot and in horse-drawn carts. Some were slain by strafing German aircraft snarling over the roads to keep them clear for advancing Wehrmacht forces. Slogging past the refugees in the opposite direction came occasional columns of captured Dutch and Belgian soldiers heading toward Germany and prisoner-of-war camps.

A fascinated and energetic witness to all this was Hugo Jaeger, a German Army photographer who took the pictures on these and the following pages. Though his perspective was that of an invader, his pictures reflect with accuracy and some sympathy the bizarre quiescence that often settles in the backwash of war.

Exuberant German artillerymen ride along a cobbled street from Holland into Belgium, their supply carts camouflaged with spring greenery.

Flames lick through the smoking ruins of a pair of houses in Rotterdam, where 814 civilians were killed in 15 minutes during a mid-May air raid.

Near Ymuiden, Holland, a freighter blown up by Dutch defense forces blocks a channel.

On a street in Brussels, broken vehicles form a hasty but unavailing barrier to Nazi tanks.

Canal water laps at a Belgian bridge destroyed by retreating troops, but German artillerymen (background) continue their advance across a temporary span.

In the quiet confusion after the blitzkrieg, German troop carriers and supply trucks speed westward along the far side of a canal near Nieuport, Belgium, while refugees' automobiles cross a pontoon bridge heading toward France. The owners of the stalled coupé at left center, flying a pair of white flags, push their car with the help of several German soldiers, as a fleeing priest totes his suitcase past a sentry in the foreground.

Tired refugees rest in a meadow, having moved away from the road to avoid the danger of being machine-gunned by German planes. While the luckier ones have carts, or even a truck (background), others have taken flight by bicycle or on foot. The little girl standing in the foreground wears her winter coat in the warm May sunlight—the most efficient way to carry the heavy garment.

A dead horse, killed by strafing aircraft, lies in a ditch, still harnessed to his cart.

133

Belgian troops, some showing a touch of stoic humor, stand with their German captors, awaiting orders to move off

to prisoner-of-war camps. Part of a regular army that numbered 700,000 at the beginning of May 1940, these men were among 200,000 who were imprisoned.

WAR CLOUDS OVER AMERICA

OUT OF WAR

S. ROOSEVELT
NGRESSMAN !

k over Here
Death over there
OR PARTY 20: A.D.

Demonstrators march at a 1940 rally in New York at which one speaker called the U.S. drift toward war an Anglo-American scheme to buoy the British pound.

THE MANY FACES OF ISOLATIONISM

The war clouds that rose over Europe cast shadows over America. Most United States citizens, including such folk heroes as Charles A. Lindbergh, wished heartily to stay out of the War. A 1939 poll showed that, although 80 per cent of Americans hoped the Allies would win, 90 per cent did not want to join the fight. As early as 1935 Congress had passed the Neutrality Act, forbidding the shipment of arms to any belligerent. When Hitler's seizure of Czechoslovakia pulled Britain and France to the brink of open conflict with Germany, President Franklin D. Roosevelt's efforts to get the Act eased were defeated. Senator Burton K. Wheeler, a devout noninterventionist, proclaimed that Roosevelt was trying to trick the United States into entering a war that would "plow under every fourth American boy." And an organization called America First enrolled 850,000 members on a platform of unflinching isolationism with the slogan, "The path to war is a false path to freedom."

In part the antiwar feeling came from a simple desire to avoid trouble. In part it reflected a traditional American dislike of foreigners and their wars. Some people specifically singled out Britain—in the words of North Dakota's Senator Gerald Nye, "the greatest aggressor in all modern history, and a bad influence on the morals of the world."

Allied with these respectable noninterventionists was an array of crackpots who supported Germany on racist or anti-Semitic grounds. The best-known of these, German émigré Fritz Kuhn, strutted in a storm trooper uniform as head of the German-American Bund, a quasi-political party that Kuhn used as a vehicle for embezzling money, chasing women and denouncing "Franklin D. Rosenfeld" as part of the "international Jewish conspiracy."

But history and logic were against the isolationists. Like it or not, the United States was linked to other democracies by ideology; more and more Americans began to agree that an attack on one was an attack on all. Slowly, the tide of isolationism ebbed; by spring 1940, polls showed that the margin had shifted, and that a majority of Americans favored active aid to their beleaguered British and French allies.

Coincidental twin signs advertise both the 1940 Presidential campaign of Wendell Willkie and a famous film satire on Hitlerism by Charlie Chaplin.

George Washington gets prominent play at a German-American Bund rally. The antiwar, anti-Semitic bundists waved swastikas and U.S. flags together.

U.S. Communist chief Earl Browder harangues an audience from a flag-draped dais at a New York Party rally in the fall of 1939 supporting the mutual-assistance pact just signed by Russia and Germany. Browder's Party line, which had been strongly anti-Nazi before the pact, turned overnight to praise for Nazi-Soviet accord and to insistence on neutrality by the United States in any European conflict. Despite Browder's eloquence, many American Communists refused to accept the switch and walked out, leaving the already weak U.S. Party all but defunct.

Smiling George Kelly gives the fighter's victory sign as he leads three fellow members of the anti-Semitic, isolationist Christian Front—and one scowling court official—from a New York courtroom in early 1940. Along with 13 other Christian Fronters, they had pleaded innocent to charges of plotting to overthrow the U.S. Government and steal arms and explosives. Though FBI chief J. Edgar Hoover insisted that they had planned to "knock off about a dozen Congressmen," the charges did not stick. Nine were acquitted, five were freed on mistrials, two were released untried, and one killed himself before his trial was completed.

Cigar-smoking William Dudley Pelley, head of the Nazi-style Silvershirt Legion of America, walks out of a Washington jail on bond pending a 1940 extradition hearing, involving a North Carolina fraud conviction. The fraud judgment was the least of the quixotic Pelley's troubles, which included an eight-year jail term—from 1942 to 1950—for advocating the overthrow of the federal government. He once proudly boasted that he and Adolf Hitler were "birds of a feather in everything."

A GROWING COMMITMENT TO THE ALLIES

As news of the war in Poland and the subsequent blitzkrieg on the Western Front flooded across the Atlantic, America began to turn away from its isolationism. The first official sign came from United States Ambassador to Berlin Hugh R. Wilson, who resigned the day Hitler's panzers entered Poland. A flurry of diplomatic correspondence followed the seizure of the U.S. freighter, *City of Flint (page 144),* by a German warship a month later.

As the country's mood began to shift, the Neutrality Act was amended to permit arms sales to combatants. And with the invasion of the Low Countries and France in the spring of 1940, popular sympathy in the United States swung heavily to the side of the Allies. Individual Americans began to involve themselves, however tentatively, in efforts to help Britain, France and the other threatened democracies. Volunteer aid and relief organizations sprang up.

Among members of the Social Register, it became fashionable to contribute time and cash to ambulance fund-raising drives for Britain, and ladies-club members by the thousands showed off new Red Cross uniforms as they rolled bandages. Others formed Molly Pitcher Brigades, so named for the Revolutionary War heroine, and trained with rifles, the better to snipe at any enemy parachutists who might drift their way. One such group in South Carolina practiced close-order drill, all the while bravely singing, "Guard our homes, our land, our young ones. Blast to hell invading wrong ones." Even the American Legion, long a pillar of isolationism, voted overwhelmingly in October 1940 to back aid for Britain.

As the old soldiers fell in line, some new faces appeared. In 10 camps throughout the country, 3,000 sober businessmen and professionals paid $43.50 apiece to spend four uncomfortable weeks in a military camp—a voluntary short-term sampling of the mass conscription to come.

On a Brooklyn pier, the shrouded fuselage of a twin-engine Lockheed bomber swings aboard a ship on the first leg of its voyage to Britain. Although 1939 amendments to the Neutrality Act theoretically permitted the sale of arms to all combatants, shipments to Germany were barred by the British naval blockade.

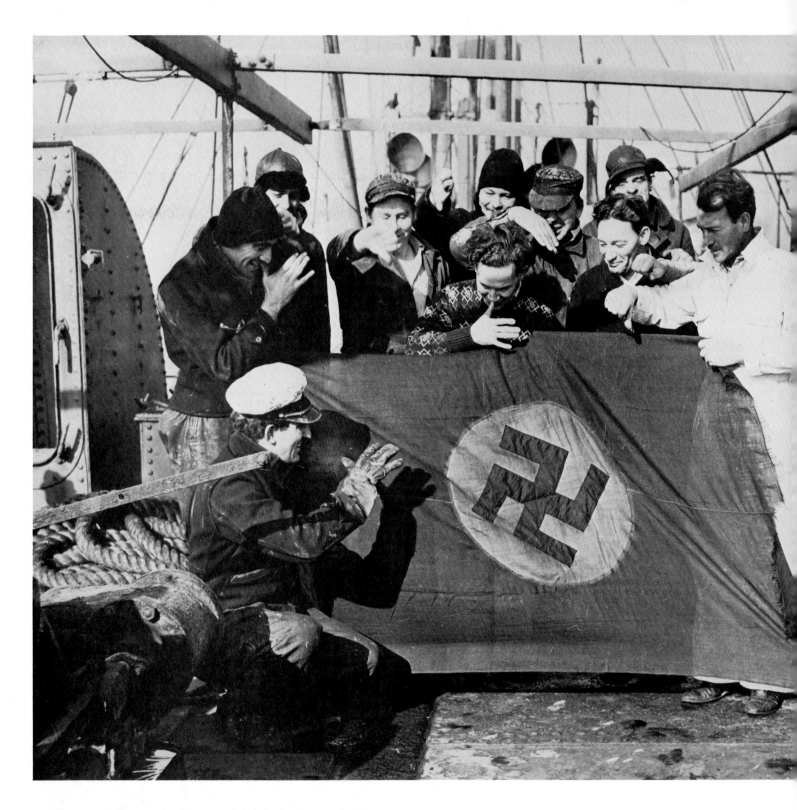

Freed crewmen of the U.S. freighter City of Flint display the swastika that
flew over their ship during much of its month-long odyssey as a German
war prize. On October 9, 1939, the Flint was seized in midocean by
the German pocket battleship Deutschland. With three German officers
and 18 German sailors aboard, the freighter headed for Germany. On
November 3, the vessel sailed into the neutral Norwegian port
of Haugesund, where her German officers wanted to get in touch with the
German Consulate. The Norwegians promptly arrested the Germans for
docking in neutral waters with a captive ship, and set the Americans free.

Mrs. Spaulding Kirkbride, Secretary of the British-American Ambulance Corps, watches as one of the 100 ambulances bought with funds the corps raised in the U.S. is eased off a train before shipment to Britain.

British-born movie stars (from left) Ronald Colman, Vivien Leigh, Laurence Olivier, Herbert Marshall and Madeleine Carroll gather at a Los Angeles radio station before joining in a broadcast for the Canadian Red Cross. The actors' voices were beamed to London via short wave, and were relayed from there to British listeners all over the world.

White-collar Americans line up in the summer of 1940 before a regular Army officer at Plattsburgh, New York. These men were some of 3,000 volunteers who showed up for a month of rudimentary training at the 10 camps run by the Military Training Camps Association, an army-sponsored organization promoting private military preparedness.

Businessmen-soldiers learn to strip and reassemble a 1917-model Browning machine gun. All modern weapons were so scarce at this time that some Plattsburgh trainees drilled with rifles that were made of wood, and were taught to operate and repair tanks that were obsolete even by the still naive and undemanding standards of 1940.

5

Even while the German panzers were grinding up the Allied armies in May 1940, the word "blitzkrieg" had meant little to Private Peter Anderson of the Royal Army Service Corps unit attached to the British 48th Division. For Anderson and his colleagues, who had the job of convoying supplies from a base near Arras in northern France to army units at the front, the early stages had been something of a lark. The closest Anderson had come to any fighting had been the occasional boom of big guns far in the distance and flights of bombers high in the sky, looking like a swarm of gnats.

Anderson, a short wiry fellow, had been a racing car mechanic before joining the service, and now he was in charge of a brand-new three-ton truck, with an assistant driver, a swaggering, blood-thirsty Scot who kept snarling "Let's go get us a bloody Hun," but didn't really mean it. They were armed with a set of maps, three hand grenades—of which Anderson was terrified—two 1914 Lee-Enfield rifles and 40 rounds of ammunition.

Their time was almost evenly divided between delivering supplies and scrounging whatever they could lay hands on for themselves, including the company of some hospitable French girls who were glad to share in their loot. On their delivery runs the men were told nothing about the rapidly disintegrating front; they were simply given map coordinates and sent off in convoy to rendezvous with other trucks from the units receiving the supplies. Then, back they would go to Base Supply, and to pleasant evenings in the cafés around the square of their headquarters village.

It was during one night in the third week in May, Anderson remembers, that his convoy was heading east, its 25 trucks loaded with food and gasoline. He was squinting carefully at the blacked-out truck ahead of him when the night exploded. There were no flashes of gunfire—only the shrill scream of shells flying overhead. It was an artillery bombardment of huge proportion, and the impact of the heavy artillery was literally earthshaking.

The truck ahead of Anderson stopped. Anderson himself stopped, and braced for the truck behind to hit his. But the convoy halted without accident, and the command went down the line: Turn off your motors; open your doors quietly; do not close them; get behind your trucks and push them; keep your mouths shut; make no noise whatever.

For the next half hour Anderson and his comrades pushed

DELIVERANCE AT DUNKIRK

their trucks along the road, grumbling and cursing in whispers. The artillery bombardment continued, but slowly the convoy rolled out of danger. Another order was passed along. Everyone climbed back into his truck; motors started, and the convoy proceeded east. Anderson guessed that the artillery was British, or perhaps French—not German. But he realized with cold fear that the fire was directed at Germans who were presumably close by. Thus he discovered that the War had finally come to him. But he knew that in this army nobody was going to tell him—or even his commanding officer, for that matter—what was going on.

If Private Anderson had been told what was happening, it would not have cheered him. On May 20 the first German panzers reached the Somme estuary at Abbeville. Immediately their armored columns started a sweep north, toward the seaports of Boulogne, Calais and Dunkirk. Boulogne fell on May 23. Calais held out for three days, then fell, while the panzers poured north toward Dunkirk.

As the pincer-arm closed in from the south, German forces broke through from the northeast. Although Belgium's army was still fighting, the way was opened for the Germans to close in on Dunkirk from the east and southeast.

A cruel decision was forced on the commander of the BEF. General Lord Gort was a brave, stubborn, intellectually limited man. His French colleagues described him condescendingly as a "jovial battalion commander"; yet his troops called him "The Tiger"—a tribute to his personal courage. His mind was all too readily bogged down by detail; at an important conference in November 1939, he had astounded his colleagues by choosing as the first subject of discussion whether a helmet, when not on a soldier's head, should be slung over the left shoulder or the right.

On balance, however, Gort was a good man for a crisis. He had the stolid character that could face up to disaster and come through it. While the top French commanders were staring in desperation at maps on the wall, Gort kept his head. As early as May 19, alarmed by the French collapse on the Meuse to his right, he had raised the possibility, in a message to London, of withdrawing the BEF to Dunkirk. The top brass in London, still believing optimistic reports from the French, sternly ordered Gort to forget about retreat.

But the general became increasingly convinced that if he were to save any of the BEF from annihilation, he must in fact retreat. And the only exit left to him was Dunkirk.

Gort's headquarters was an unpretentious stone château at Premesques, near Lille. For most of the afternoon of the 23rd he sat alone at his trestle-table desk in the château's drawing room. He knew that a decision to retreat would be contrary to orders not only from London but also from his French superior, General Weygand. He had been told to attack the German forces to the south, in hopes of stalling their drive. But Gort was convinced that such a counterattack would be ultimately useless, even if it brought momentary success. Earlier that morning, after his breakfast of hard biscuits and marmalade, he had confided to an aide: "You know, the day I joined up, I never thought I'd lead the British Army to its biggest defeat in history." By 6 o'clock Gort's mind was made up. He would pull back from the south, and start defending a corridor of retreat.

The decision that saved the BEF was thus made. The army would not fight its way south in a last attempt to stop the blitzkrieg, but north and east, heading to Dunkirk, to the Channel and—God willing—to England. His mind made up, Gort went for his customary two-mile walk and returned for one sherry, a meagre dinner and bed.

The great question was: Could the BEF make it? At the time of Gort's decision the Germans were much closer to Dunkirk than the BEF were. But what made Gort's decision the right one—though of course he could not know it—was the fact that the Germans chose, unwittingly, to help him by making strategic mistakes. The chief error was made by Hitler himself. Despite the heroic defenses of Boulogne and Calais, Guderian's panzers found themselves almost in sight of Dunkirk by May 24. They were halted by the Aa Canal, 30 yards wide, a scant 12 miles from Dunkirk, the last tank obstacle in Guderian's way.

By the morning of the 25th, pontoon bridges were spanning the canal. A few tanks were across, roaring and throbbing as their crews waited for the rest of the panzer division to form up. But the order to advance was held up—that day and the next—by the intercession of Hitler.

On May 24, the Führer had visited General Gerd von Rundstedt, Guderian's commander, at the GHQ of Army Group A at Charleville, in the Ardennes, to review the heady reports of German progress. As on frequent previous occasions, it was a surprise visit. An orderly scarcely had time to open Rundstedt's window and clear the tobacco smoke that Hitler could not abide; a staff officer quickly dumped his Cointreau bottles—another of Hitler's aversions—into a filing cabinet. The Führer's big black Mercedes, its top down, rolled up to the ivy-covered townhouse that was Rundstedt's headquarters. The Führer, in his brown jacket and riding breeches, stepped out of the back seat, flipped his salute and walked into the building.

The group gathered around the operations map while Rundstedt reviewed the situation. Then Hitler, acting partly on Rundstedt's urging, made a decision which, like Gort's, changed the course of World War II. He ordered the tanks stopped at the Aa Canal.

Historians have puzzled over this decision ever since. When one more day of advance could have brought the German tanks sweeping down on Dunkirk to close off the last exit for the BEF, why did Hitler stop them?

The most likely reason for the decision to halt the tanks was simply in order to conserve them. Throughout the race across France and Belgium, Hitler had worried about the panzers' long thin spearheads and flanks exposed to a possible slicing counterattack.

The Führer felt that victory was certain if they took their time to make sure of it—step by step. The tanks that had made this victory possible should not now be expended where they were not needed; they should be husbanded for bigger battles to come. After all, the rest of France remained to be conquered. The goal, in the end, was Paris, not an unimpressive port city like Dunkirk. If gaining that goal meant that some British soldiers would manage to escape across the Channel, it was a small price to pay. And Göring's air force could play an important part in minimizing the number of soldiers who escaped.

The stop order infuriated Guderian. From a hill near Dunkirk he could see the rooftops of the town, and he could imagine the hasty preparations for snatching thousands of enemy troops from his grasp and the hordes pouring down the roads toward the last exit from northern Europe.

Contrary to appearances, however, the soldiers on the roads were not the vanguard of a rout, though the retreat to Dunkirk was not without confusion at all levels of the Allied forces. After Gort's decision was implemented—with, by now, approval from London—the French High Command was still talking about counterattacks to drive the Germans back from the coast. On May 28, two days after London had informed General Weygand of the decision to retreat, Weygand's field commander, General Georges Blanchard, had not received the news. When Gort informed him, Blanchard was appalled, as was Gort that Blanchard did not know.

The French generals asked for another day—24 fatal hours for the French First Army, which then found itself surrounded. Its men gallantly held out for three more days before about half of them surrendered. But the other half did manage to reach Dunkirk, along with hundreds of thousands of British and remnants of the Belgian Army.

Civilians mingled with the soldiers on the roads to the port. All found themselves in the line of fire. One marcher was an eight-year-old boy, holding his sister's hand and pulling a box on wheels containing a few belongings. A German plane roared down on the road, stitching it with machine-gun fire. Boy, sister and wagon tumbled into the ditch. Then, expressionless, the boy helped his sister back onto the road, righted the wagon, and they went on their way.

Swept up in the retreat were Private Anderson and his fellow truckers from the 48th, which was still delivering supplies. Their convoy routes were shorter now that the front was closing in; everyone pretty much knew that the army was heading toward Dunkirk to attempt an escape by sea. Like many other soldiers, these animal-loving Britons had mascots that they had freed from abandoned houses. Anderson's truck carried two cats and a canary in an uneasy truce. Others carried dogs, sheep and goats that they had picked up along the way.

In the atmosphere of defeat, the concept of private property lost much of its peacetime sanctity; everyone had abandoned home and belongings. In a shattered shop window on a deserted village street Anderson found a pair of riding boots and three pairs of corduroy trousers. Some of his friends collected jewelry. One member of the company, a clumsy fellow with a bad stutter, collected toys, which he handed out to the children whom he encountered along the way. In a farm house Anderson and his friends found an overlooked cellar full of cheese, cream, bread and wine. They moved a table to the side of the road, and passed out jugs of cheese, chamber pots full of cream and loaves of bread to the people pouring by. They kept the wine, and put it in their trucks for safekeeping.

Each day the strafing increased. The agile bombers would come in at a shallow, shrieking dive, spray the road, make a tight climbing turn, and come back from the opposite direction. Anderson and his friends would dive for the ditch and hope that their trucks would not catch fire from a bullet in the gas tank. Sometimes they passed burned-out vehicles, some with blackened bodies still in the front seats or lying half out of the open doors; the air carried the nauseating stench of burnt flesh, rubber and wiring. For Anderson, the spirit of adventure had given way to fear. In a night bivouac, he found himself on guard duty, armed with a heavy Bren gun, a hardy automatic rifle that could be set to fire either single shots or bursts. He hated guns, and he had never mastered their use. Now, as he tried to make out the countryside around him in the darkness, he could not tell what scared him more—the Bren or the unseen peril around him.

As he watched, something moved along a hedge to his left. He reached for the gun. The movement stopped. There it was again, just beyond the hedge and closer to his post.

By the rules Anderson should have called out: "Who goes there?" Instead, he shouldered the gun and gave a quick nudge to the trigger to get off a warning shot. In the split second that his finger was on the trigger, the Bren gun, with an ear-shattering splatter, sprayed the dark hedge. Everywhere around him the air filled with cries and screams, and running feet thudded through the bivouac.

At that point Anderson realized that the screaming, running men were his own; that his Bren gun had been set for bursts instead of single shots; and that he had all but bisected a cow. He was reprimanded half-heartedly by the major commanding his unit, who repeated his long-held belief that Anderson would never make a soldier; but he was permitted to share in the steaks he had provided.

They even had enough steaks to hand out a few to the members of other units streaming west. They wished the

German motorcyclists halt momentarily on a road in northern France to get their bearings from maps. In the vanguard of the blitzkrieg, such cyclists roared ahead of panzer columns and motorized infantry outfits to check out roads, locate enemy troop dispositions and relay the information back to main units.

men good luck and assured them, without really knowing, that there would be ships waiting for them at Dunkirk.

At Dover, along the Thames River and dozens of rivers and estuaries indenting the east coast of England, the sound of boats could be heard through the last week of May. There had been a crackling air of expectancy along the coast for days, as the bad news kept coming in from the Continent. So the people who woke to hear the thrumming of the boats' engines knew what it meant.

As early as May 20, the Navy had started planning what it called *Operation Dynamo*. No one knew how many of the men in the BEF would reach an escape port; but it was obvious that rescuing them would require every vessel that could be found. The operation would have to take place in a desperately short time and under battle conditions.

Destroyers were perhaps the best vessels for such an operation. They were fast and could make more round trips per day. They had effective armament to fight off dive-bombers. But of the British Navy's 200 destroyers and escorts, only 41 were available; the rest were sunk, in repair, needed for Channel defense work or scattered around the world. So every other type of vessel was commandeered as well, including personnel ships, fishing trawlers, fireboats, ancient paddle-wheelers and lumbering old Thames River barges, with their stubby masts and enormous canvas sails. French, Dutch and Belgian vessels raced to the scene.

In addition, the call went out to every yacht club along the coast, and yachtsmen converged from everywhere. Some relinquished their prized boats to the Navy, but many insisted on joining the operation themselves.

Nor were the yachtsmen the only volunteers. When the Navy requisitioned the 70-ton Swedish-built motor vessel *Bee* at Portsmouth, her engineer, Fred Reynard, refused to leave his engine room. Called before the local naval commander, Admiral Sir William James, Reynard said, "Beg pardon, sir, what do your young gentlemen know about Swedish engines? I've been looking after them since 1912."

Sir William explained. "We've no guarantee you'll get back," he said. "Ever been under shellfire?"

Reynard threw back his shoulders. "Ever heard of Gallipoli?" The admiral had indeed heard of this terrible battle of World War I, and Reynard sailed with the *Bee*.

The armada that set forth on May 26 presented an unbelievable sight. Stacked three deep along the Dover quays, like people in a pub, were motor launches and sloops, fishing boats and schooners.

Pouring out of Folkestone, Margate, Portsmouth and Ramsgate was a fleet whose infinite variety had never been seen before and probably never would be seen again: the Yangtze gun boat *Mosquito;* a Thames barge named *Galleon's Reach;* the cross-Channel ferry *Canterbury;* the island ferry *Gracie Fields;* the launch *Count Dracula,* once owned by a German admiral, scuttled at Scapa Flow in 1919 and later salvaged by the British; Tom Sopwith's America's Cup challenger *Endeavour;* the century-old open sailboat *Dumpling.* The skippers were as diverse as their boats were: the yacht *Sundowner's* owner, Commander C. H. Lightoller, who had been the senior surviving officer aboard the *Titanic;* the Honorable Lionel Lambert, who had armed his yacht and brought along his private chef; the Earl of Craven serving as a third engineer aboard the tug *St. Olaf;* 67-year-old Captain "Potato" Jones, who, belying his bland nickname, had run Franco's blockades with his *Marie Llewellyn* during the civil war in Spain, and who wore a ring in his ear.

The Channel crossing was as much an ordeal as the corridor through which the soldiers were fleeing in France. In

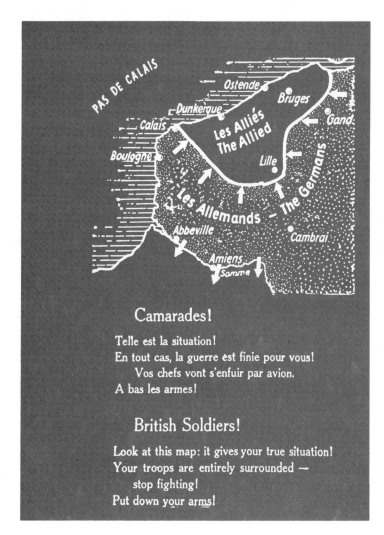

Camarades!

Telle est la situation!
En tout cas, la guerre est finie pour vous!
Vos chefs vont s'enfuir par avion.
A bas les armes!

British Soldiers!

Look at this map: it gives your true situation!
Your troops are entirely surrounded —
stop fighting!
Put down your arms!

In May 1940, German planes dropped leaflets like these, playing upon the predicament of British, French and Belgian troops in the fast-shrinking Dunkirk defense perimeter. The map accurately showed the Allied forces completely encircled by German troops. Despite the German demand that fighting cease, the encircled troops did not give up; instead, they hurriedly fortified the contracting lines to buy time for evacuation by sea.

the open Channel the lighted buoys and lightships were blacked out. The Channel waters were heavily mined, and the British Navy had swept only three narrow passageways to the Continent. And as the first contingent of skippers discovered, there were other lethal hazards: the Germans had already moved big guns against Calais, and swept enormous areas of the Channel with shellfire.

The dive bombers were worst of all. As the ships crept between the shoals just off Dunkirk, they were like sitting ducks. They could not speed up; there was not enough sea room in the narrow approaches to Dunkirk for evasive action. Those skippers who tried to make their run at too great a speed in order to dodge the dive bombers and artillery shells ran aground on the sand banks. Their hulks posed a further menace for the following ships.

Yet somehow hundreds of vessels did get through—not only to the harbor and its beach, but to outlying beaches north and south of the town. Before they came within sight of Dunkirk, their skippers found that the Germans had provided them with an unmistakable beacon: a billowing smoke signal from Dunkirk's oil tanks, ignited by the dive-bombing Stukas and the guns around the perimeter.

Indeed, inside Dunkirk everything seemed to be on fire. Yet Dunkirk's flames also helped make the evacuation possible. By day the billowing clouds of smoke covered the city, and many waves of dive bombers returned to their bases without attacking; they couldn't find targets. By night the fires illuminated the harbor entrance and the few quays and warehouses that had not been reduced to wreckage.

Most of them already had been destroyed; the only harborside structure where the big transports could dock was one of the two breakwaters enclosing the harbor itself. This jetty was a mole, two thirds of a mile long, constructed of rock, with thick pilings alongside it; the swells of the open Channel rushed against it and sucked and swirled through the rocks. Most of its surface was boarded over, with a railing of timber along the edges, forming a gangplank that was sufficiently sturdy, but only wide enough for men to pass three abreast. The tides rose and fell 15 feet; at high tide men walked across makeshift bridges onto ships' decks—one ingenious ship's carpenter made spans out of water polo goal posts. At low tide they had to jump from the mole.

From the vessels making fast, the sight of the men waiting along the top of the mole was never to be forgotten by anyone. The line stretched the length of the mole and back along the beach in one endless serpentine mass. The troops were in every state of disarray. Their gaunt, unshaven faces were expressionless with exhaustion. Some were supporting others too tired to stand any longer.

When the planes came in over Dunkirk, the men on the mole could not take cover; they could only lie flat and watch the lines of bullets splatter across the harbor toward them —"crackling like frying fat," as one man remembered.

As the planes swept over them and climbed away, their bombs churned the harbor and smashed into the ships. During one of the most devastating raids a bomb went into the paddle-wheel steamer *Fenella*, which had just loaded 600 troops. Many of them were killed instantly. Another bomb hit the jetty and sent missiles of concrete and rock through the *Fenella's* hull beneath the waterline. The engine room was wrecked, and the hold began to fill with water. With their section of the mole destroyed, the *Fenella's* crew evacuated the remaining troops off the stern, some able to jump and run for it, some carried on stretchers. Enemy fighters machine-gunned them, but most made it to the *Crested Eagle*, another paddle steamer alongside the jetty.

The destroyer *Grenade*, at the mole with the others, was set afire; her mooring lines burned away and she drifted out of control into the fairway, blocking the harbor entrance. A trawler raced out to her and, despite the flames and explosions, got a line onto her and towed the burning hulk away from the harbor entrance.

Past the smoldering wreckage chugged the paddle steamer *Crested Eagle* with the refugees from the *Fenella* and her own complement of survivors. Another dive bomber swung down on her. The *Crested Eagle* burst into flame and drifted onto the beach; most of the troops died in the fire.

As these vessels burned and sank, their wreckage turned the harbor into an obstacle course. But the ships still came. The troops still shuffled down the mole. And they continued the evacuation. Stolidly, stubbornly, the skippers ran the fiery gauntlet, sometimes even having a moment of revenge. Captain R. Duggan, master of the packet boat *Mona's Queen*, later described the holocaust in which his ship was riddled with shrapnel from the shore batteries and attacked by a dive bomber. The guns on the ships around him swung toward the dive bomber and hit it. Duggan reported that it "crashed into the water just ahead of us. Then another Junkers attacked us, but before he reached us he was brought down in flames. Then the tension eased a little. Owing to the bombardment, I could see that the nerves of some of my men were badly shaken. I did not feel too well myself."

Aboard some ships there were so many men on deck that the guns could not be worked. One of the smaller ships tied up to a quay in the harbor and took on so many troops that the vessel slowly sank to the bottom. The men clambered back onto the quay. At low tide the crew salvaged the ship and dried out and repaired her engines, and she left Dunkirk with 300 men.

But it was Commander Lightoller, the officer who had escaped from the *Titanic,* who set some kind of record for the number of passengers aboard a pleasure craft. Lightoller, using antiquated charts, and with only his son and a Sea Scout as a crew, crossed the Channel where, dodging the dive bombers, he sailed into Dunkirk harbor. Warping his 60-foot *Sundowner* alongside a destroyer at the mole, he began to take on troops. As the men went below, he instructed them to lie down. After 50 men had come aboard, he called below to his son, "How are you getting on?" His son called back, "Oh, plenty of room yet." When the number reached 75, his son confessed that it was getting crowded in the cabin. As the soldiers still poured aboard, Lightoller told them to go forward and lie down on deck. "By the time we had 50 on deck," he recalled, "I could feel her getting distinctly tender"—a seaman's term for a difficult-to-handle vessel. Carrying a total of 130 men, and with fighters snarling around her, the *Sundowner* ran for England.

When Lightoller brought his yacht alongside a quay at Ramsgate, the 60-foot *Sundowner* rolled wildly as everyone got to his feet at once. But she righted and as the many refugees swarmed ashore, Lightoller remembered that "the look on the official face was amusing to behold." A stoker who helped the men ashore shook his head in amazement and asked, "God's truth, mate! Where did you put them?"

Despite such successes, however, had it been only the mole and the few serviceable quays in Dunkirk that were used for loading the BEF's human cargo, not many would have made it home. In addition to the long line snaking out onto the mole, there were other lines on the harbor beach itself. Captain R. B. Brett of the minesweeper *Medway Queen* recalled later that, as he neared the shore, he saw what appeared to be a causeway about eight feet wide extending into the water. "To my surprise," he wrote, "I found it to be a perfectly ordered straight column of men, about six abreast, standing as if on parade." The men at the head of the column were in water to their necks.

Many of the men on the beach still had their pets. But most of the skippers, like Captain R. Hughes of the personnel ship *Killarney,* felt obliged to lay down the law against animals. Some of the soldiers, concluding that their pets would starve to death, used their last ammunition to shoot them before leaving the beach. One BEF officer, Captain Edward Bloom, had adopted a huge sled dog and had named him Hugo. Bloom always remembered how he took Hugo behind one of the dunes and talked soothingly to him for a few minutes before shooting him.

A German soldier snapped this grim tableau of a Dunkirk beach littered with casualties, wrecked vehicles, artillery pieces and ammunition boxes, shortly after panzer units finally succeeded in smashing through Allied lines. Ironically, the scenes became grim for German commanders, too, when they discovered that while most of the British and French forces' equipment had been captured, the bulk of the troops had escaped by sea.

The troops taken aboard the *Killarney* had an eventful voyage home. Her decks packed with men, she ran into a bombardment from German shore batteries. For nearly an hour the shelling continued, while Captain Hughes tried to zigzag in the narrow passages between the shoals. One direct hit on the *Killarney's* stern killed eight men and wounded 30. The ship was hardly out of artillery range when she was attacked by a dive bomber. But a British Spitfire appeared and drove the Germans away. Finally free to run for home, the *Killarney* had to heave to again, this time to pick up some men afloat on a raft made of a door and scrap lumber: they were three Belgians and a Frenchman, carrying two tins of biscuits, six demijohns of wine and a bicycle.

It was much quieter on the outlying beaches immediately north and south of Dunkirk. The crackling, exploding fires of the city could be heard in the distance, and the shells arched over the southern beaches before descending on Dunkirk. The men formed orderly lines, as they did on the

mole, then sat on the sand and quietly waited. Sapper Thomas Morley, coming over the rise of the back dunes near Dunkirk on the evening of May 29, wondered at the thousands of pin points of light; it looked like a field of fireflies. As he walked down into the sand, he realized that each pin point represented a man, smoking his cigarette as he waited for his line to edge closer to the beach.

The smaller vessels were sent to these outlying beaches —Malo-les-Bains, Bray Dunes and La Panne to the north and Mardyck to the south. In some ways it was no easier here than along the jetty at Dunkirk; the Channel tides uncovered half a mile of beach at low water. The shore shelved so gradually that even the shallower-draft vessels had to heave to hundreds of yards off the beach. Tide rips swirled around and over the sand banks.

And the Stukas did not neglect the beaches. Huddling behind a rise at Bray Dunes and watching one wave of shrieking dive bombers swoop over the boats off the shore, Private Charles Ginnever found himself muttering, "Oh, I hand it to you, Jerry—you're the best, the cream." Soon the oil slicks from the wreckage were smearing the shoreline, making a slippery mess of the rescue work.

The coasters, lifeboats and yachts came in as close as they dared. But in many places it was not close enough. Men in their heavy uniforms waded out, tried to swim and were dragged to the bottom by their wet clothes.

Some men tried to build makeshift piers from the frames of trucks, wreckage and driftwood. But one skipper had a better idea: he decided to make his boat into a temporary pier. On May 29, Lieutenant E. L. Davies aimed his paddle-minesweeper *Oriole* at the beach above Dunkirk, ordered his crew aft to raise the bow as high as possible, and sent her at 12 knots for the beach, dropping two anchors astern as they went in. Nearly 3,000 troops waded out to the beached *Oriole* and used her as a bridge to deeper water where other craft could take them off her stern. That night at flood tide everyone bent to the anchor lines and helped haul the *Oriole* off the sand bar. She returned to England with 700 soldiers and nurses from a field hospital.

Some ships had brought collapsible boats. They sent them ashore and thousands of soldiers escaped in them, paddling with gun butts and bailing with helmets. But many others were drowned when these light boats capsized in the surf. And those who did get hauled aboard the ships still faced danger from planes. More than 700 men had just settled down with relief in the cabins and on the deck of the paddle-minesweeper *Gracie Fields* when a dive bomber got her. The pipes burst in her engine room, and no one could go below to stop her engines. Her rudder jammed and the *Gracie Fields* went into a tight circle at six knots. Two tugs and another minesweeper managed to swing alongside and circle with her while taking off the survivors.

Incidents like these were multiplied by the thousands. Despite the planes and the artillery, the mines and the shoals, nearly 900 ships kept going back and forth across the Channel, and they brought more than 200,000 troops of the BEF home to England. By the end of May, Dover was overflowing with them; yet for some reason it never occurred to the Germans to bomb that city.

On the Continent the few remaining troops continued to close the perimeter around Dunkirk, slowly and stubbornly, while the ships completed their evacuation. Among the last to go were Gort and the French commander, Admiral Abrial. On the night of June 2—the Germans were so close by now that daylight evacuation was impossible—the last substantial units of British troops left. There was more space in the boats than they needed, and thousands more French might have joined them that night; but through another breakdown of communications no one had told them.

This was supposed to be the end of *Operation Dynamo*. But the rear guard on the perimeter went on fighting more courageously and effectively than anyone had anticipated. On the night of June 3 the Royal Navy sent its exhausted crews back for another sweep, and took off more than 26,000 French soldiers. Rescuing them was in many cases a hazardous task because of language difficulties. Time and again, too many Frenchmen would swarm into a lifeboat and capsize it, unable to comprehend the boatswain's orders to climb aboard one by one. As a result, other Frenchmen refused to wade into the surf to reach the boats. One French officer stubbornly remained on the beach, and when the skipper of the rescue yacht sent a man in to get him, the Frenchman sent out a note. The skipper translated it: "I have just eaten and am therefore unable to enter the water."

During that same day Private Peter Anderson and the 48th Division had made their final convoy run from the outskirts of the city into Dunkirk, with food for the last of the waiting troops. His last orders were to take his truck back to the outskirts, feed any troops still arriving until his supplies gave out, and then head down to one of the beaches to board any rescue craft he could find.

He left his truck at Bray Dunes, stripping the gears and smashing the engine as he had been ordered to do. He abandoned his rifle, which he felt he no longer needed, his tin hat, which had never fitted him, and his scuffed army boots. He replaced his uniform breeches with the corduroy trousers he had found in the deserted shop window, pulled on the riding boots he had found at the same place, put on a forage cap he had found somewhere else, and put a few of his treasures, including the two other pairs of corduroy trousers, into his pack. Then he strolled down through the dunes.

There were still lines of men on this beach, some of whom delighted Anderson by mistaking him for an officer in his new boots. Offshore destroyers were running back and forth; they reminded Anderson of strutting officers. Some smaller vessels were lying to, and lifeboats were coming in to fill up with men wading through a gentle surf. Anderson walked about enjoying the scene. It looked as if all he had to do was be patient, and he would be taken off; there was no need to join one of the lines quite yet. It was pleasant June weather. The sand was white and powdery. And there was no sign of the enemy—only the rolling clouds of smoke over Dunkirk off to his left.

Then someone called to him by name. Behind a dune sat a convivial group from Base Supply. There was Green, a jovial, obese fellow; "Rabbit," a diminutive sergeant so-called for his eating mannerisms; Gill, a grumpy corporal who rarely took his pipe from his mouth, and usually lost his false uppers when he did. With them were a couple of strangers. Anderson was welcomed to the group on condition that he supply a water bottle full of liquor; each of the others had done so, and were not interested in sharing theirs. There was a source of supply, they explained, in an abandoned restaurant fronting the sea a short distance away. Anderson found the place, but the only strong drink left consisted of a few bottles of Cointreau. He filled his canteen with the sweet liqueur and returned to his friends.

The group spent a pleasant, mildly alcoholic afternoon

and evening in their outpost tucked behind the beach. Next morning, however, the shooting war was on again.

As Anderson and his companions watched from behind their dune, the Stukas and Messerschmitts shrieked over the beach and scattered waiting men. Other planes dive-bombed the destroyers, which went into evasive action and opened up with their deck guns. Anderson remembers gasping as he saw a plane dive at a destroyer and seem to hover over it; there was a blinding flash and then nothing but churning water where the destroyer had been. Shortly another destroyer was hit in the stern. It settled into the water backwards, and was gone in minutes.

Intermittently the attacks went on. The troops would line up, then hit the sand or run as another wave came over, then line up again. At one point six planes swept the beach; the troops raced for cover, then came out cheering at the planes, which bore the colored circles of the RAF. With the men waving at them, the planes made a tight turn and swept the beach again, cutting the men down like scythed grass. They were captured planes piloted by Germans.

All day a hospital ship, with big red crosses on its side, rode at anchor off the beach. It survived the air attacks: Anderson could not tell whether or not it was because the dive bombers were respecting the red crosses. But late in the afternoon the ship was attacked. A bomb went down her funnel. There was a moment in which Anderson thought the bomb had missed; and then the upper decks disintegrated. The rest of the ship erupted in flame, and what looked from the beach like a blanket of ants swarmed over the side into the water. By dusk the bodies were washing up on the beach; the waiting men laid capes and coats over the bodies and left them there. Through the night the hospital ship continued to burn, and in the light from its fire the covered bodies looked to Anderson like huge jellyfish, beached by the tide and still quivering on the sand.

By dawn of June 5, there were still a great many men remaining on the beach. And the rescue boats had gone. By evening, Anderson's group had run out of liquid sustenance, but they found some barely edible chocolate bars, and settled down patiently to wait and hope. Perhaps the night would bring the rescue ships back.

Shortly they noticed that a group of men, led by a captain, were engaged in trying to reach one of the lifeboats that had been stranded on the sand bars. Anderson and his friends asked to join the operation. They brought back one ship's lifeboat, big enough to carry about 40 men. They readied it for use and retired to the dunes to await darkness before setting out to sea.

Later that afternoon a shout went up as a big paddle steamer hove into view and stood by right off their beach. Anderson's group raced for their lifeboat and pushed it into the water. Anderson tried to climb in, but was impeded by his pack. It carried his precious loot, including those two extra pairs of corduroy trousers. But he jettisoned the pack and clambered into one of the last spaces in the lifeboat.

When the boat reached the looming side of the paddle steamer, Anderson climbed a rope netting, watching his fat friend Green struggle to make it, eyes bulging and lungs heaving as he clung to the netting for his life.

The boat went back and forth until the beach was empty and the steamer was full. She was the *Margate Belle*; and when her huge paddles churned up the sea as she headed for England, Anderson went below and collapsed. He slept all the way across the Channel, waking only when the *Margate Belle* creaked into her regular berth at Margate, just as if she had completed an uneventful peacetime crossing.

Meanwhile, the pocket around Dunkirk had shrunk to nothing. The rear guard headquarters staff had come out on the mole to ships that had slipped in to evacuate them, getting the last staff members off at 2 a.m. on June 4. Later that day the Germans entered the city.

They found the jetty still packed with French troops. It was slow work turning them around and marching them off as prisoners. While this was going on, a French navy doctor, who was near the end of the jetty, noticed what looked like a perfectly good lifeboat aboard a ship that had sunk right in front of him. He recruited 12 daredevils among the men packed around him. They leaped aboard the ship, launched the lifeboat and got its pedal-operated propeller going; then they pedaled furiously away under a rain of German machine-gun bullets. Once out of range the doctor and his companions improvised a sail out of a blanket. Hours later, they were picked up at sea by a naval vessel and brought safely to England, the last of 338,226 British, French, Belgian and Dutch troops to escape from Dunkirk.

RUSHING TO AN ARMY'S RESCUE

British Tommies crowd the 1900-vintage paddle-minesweeper Emperor of India, *one of hundreds of craft that took Allied troops off the French beachhead.*

DOWN TO THE SEA IN WHATEVER WOULD FLOAT

Motorboats, requisitioned by the British Admiralty, are towed down the Thames to join other small craft bound across the Channel for Dunkirk.

From the deck of the steamer *Shamrock*, heading to Dunkirk to pick up survivors of the Allied armies on May 30, 1940, the scene on shore was at first incomprehensible. "We stared and stared," the skipper later wrote, "at what looked like thousands of sticks on the beach, and were amazed to see them turn into moving masses of humanity."

The mass was some 300,000 French and British troops —squeezed into a seven-mile-wide perimeter around the French port by advancing Germans. Despite the awful danger, the men on the beach remained surprisingly calm during the nine days between the arrival of the first rescue ship and the final German breakthrough that sealed off the beaches. On one pier, men fell in three abreast under fire; as their officer snapped, "Front rank, one pace forward. Jump!" they leaped with parade precision onto the deck of a barge 15 feet below. With the beach exploding around them, Yorkshire infantrymen bellowed such songs as "Oh, I *do* like to be by the seaside." In the same mood, a sailor guiding troops aboard his boat mimicked a peacetime excursion tout: "Any more," he bawled, "for the *Brighton Queen?*"

There were, of course, exceptions to the prevailing order and humor. A British major, nerves ragged after days of combat, bucked a line of men boarding a boat and tried to climb in. When he seemed about to swamp the already overcrowded boat, its commander shot him dead. But such incidents were mercifully few. Virtually all of the evacuation casualties came either from German bombs and shells on the beach, or from the sinking of rescue ships. For example, the paddle-minesweeper *Brighton Belle* fouled a sunken wreck and went down. The French destroyer *Bourrasque* struck a magnetic mine and sank, killing several hundred.

However, to the amazement of the Allies—and the frustration of the besieging Germans—almost all the evacuees reached Britain. There they were welcomed by friendly English faces, strong tea and a chance to forget the War—if only for a few days. But one weary seaman was not allowed to forget at all. As he arrived home, his pet parrot greeted him: "Where have you been, Fred, eh?"

Tommies watch as a line of their comrades, some chest-deep in the sea, wade out toward a transport anchored well off the shallow beach.

Calm but weary troopers scramble aboard a destroyer docked at East Mole, a narrow pier in Dunkirk harbor. Despite high winds, tide rips and incessant bombing and strafing by Luftwaffe planes, 200,000 men embarked from the Mole. "All the accumulated strain of the last few hours, of the last day or so vanished," said an army officer after boarding a ship. "Anything else that remained to be done was the Navy's business."

At a quay in England, a flotilla of destroyers ties up to disembark soldiers. Once ashore the men were greeted by eager civilian volunteers who tried to provide them with a little cheer and comfort—including postcards so that soldiers would be able to notify their families of their safe arrival.

Tommies just back from Dunkirk walk along a quay next to a railroad car. For the pair in the foreground, borrowed clothes and a blanket replace wet uniforms.

Fishing boats loaded with French troops prepare to disembark their human cargo in Britain. In nine days of frantic shuttling back and forth between English ports and Dunkirk, 338,226 Allied troops were rescued.

French soldiers, some already writing home about their Dunkirk ordeal, relax on railroad tracks beside an English pier before being sent to inland relocation camps.

French marines and soldiers of the Dunkirk rear
guard take hot tea from a laughing matron in a
southern English post. These men were the last
to have pulled out of the beleaguered
beachhead in France; 44,000 of their French
and English comrades had to be left behind
—and were killed or captured by the Germans.

ARYANS BY THE TON

Sculptor Josef Thorak models an idealized head of Hitler in a studio jammed with heroic statuary and busts of other notables.

A NATION'S ART RETOOLED FOR WAR

The 1940 granite bas-relief carved by Arno Breker for a building projected —but never built—in Berlin, symbolizes a Germany rising from defeat.

Perhaps the most confident, and surely the most effective, art critic in all history was Adolf Hitler. When he ruled the Reich, he was volubly certain of what he liked in painting and sculpture—and what he liked was what Germany got. Hitler's taste ran heavily to contrived, propagandistic art where heroic or occasionally homey Germans were shown in their prescribed roles as Nordic superfolk, dedicated to country, hearth and order. Like many an art critic, Hitler was a failed painter infatuated with the kinds of works that he had admired in his youth: representative renderings of classic figures—many of them nude—in allegorical motifs or in rustic settings. To Hitler, the cubists, surrealists and other innovators who painted blue meadows and yellow clouds belonged in mental hospitals or in jail.

With these standards held firmly up front, Hitler sent German art goose-stepping back into the 19th Century. Works of modernists such as Van Gogh, Gauguin, Picasso, Chagall and Modigliani were pulled down from museum walls and sold abroad; some 5,000 less marketable paintings were burned. Simultaneously, Hitler created an art bureaucracy that assembled lists of German artists whose work met Hitler's criteria. Those who were on the lists were free to paint whatever the Führer liked. They enjoyed total immunity from bad reviews; in fact Propaganda Minister Joseph Goebbels banned all negative art criticism. And Hitler's particular favorites were exempted from military service.

Among those whom the Führer particularly approved were sculptors like Arno Breker and Josef Thorak, whose slick busts and outsized statuary frequently dominated the annual shows at Munich's massive House of German Art —where Hitler's imprimatur was required for each exhibit. The field also included painters such as Adolf Wissel, a specialist in rendering loyally industrious peasants, and Sepp Hilz and Adolf Zeigler, whose discreetly sexy oils spiced the exhibitions with officially sanctioned nudity. All celebrated the new mission of the German artist: to reawaken Teutonic racial pride, to turn that pride toward total war, and when war came, to sustain the nation's nationalistic spirit.

Heedless of a clinging Venus, a dutiful and Teutonic Adonis springs to arms in this 1924 allegory by Arthur Kampf, whose career throve during the Nazi era.

The 1936 limestone sentinel above, by sculptor Willy Meller, confronted pupils at the Ordensburg Vogelsang, one of four training schools for prospective Nazi leaders. "You are the torch-bearers of the nation," adjures the inscription. "You carry before you the light of the spirit in the name of Adolf Hitler."

Arno Breker touches up one of his more restrained works, a bust of Hitler's favorite architect, Albert Speer. Many other Breker sculptures were the same sort of huge figures endowed with exaggerated musculature, even more idealized than were the productions of his colleague Josef Thorak at right. Unable to find live Germans who were sufficiently developed to serve as models, Breker had to fall back on anatomy texts for guidance.

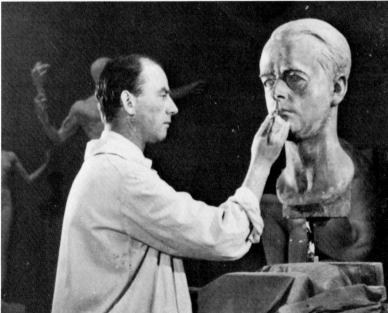

ALLEMAGNE

Both the almost 20-foot-high family group above and the similarly scaled "Comradeship" at left were produced by the prolific sculptor Josef Thorak. He carved the defiant trio for exhibit in the German pavilion at the 1937 World's Fair in Paris, and the bronze comrades dominated the opening, in the same year, of Munich's House of German Art, scene of the most prestigious of Nazi exhibitions. Like Breker, Thorak was a World War I veteran—which may have helped to ingratiate him with old soldier Hitler. When Nazi investigators unearthed a Communist manifesto that had been signed by Thorak in his youth, Hitler lightly dismissed the discovery with a surprising and paternal commentary on the artist as activist: "Artists are simple-hearted souls," he said. "Today they sign this, tomorrow that."

NAKED PENELOPES
THAT PLEASED A PRUDE

Like herbs in a hearty stew, nudes were sprinkled through the inspirational processions of heroic statuary at Nazi art shows to make the shows more palatable, and to help pull people in off the street to look at the less toothsome works. The nudity was somewhat out of keeping in the militantly strait-laced Germany of the 1930s. But nobody protested, not even the otherwise prudish Adolf Hitler, whose acceptance of some explicit nude oils startled even the cynical Dr. Goebbels.

Such acceptance, however, depended entirely upon the painters' adherence to the Führer's concepts of how a nude woman ought to be represented. The rules specified that she be neat and clean, with full breasts, flat belly, long-muscled thighs and slim shanks—the ideologically scrubbed, virginal image of Nordic maidenhood. And so long as the painter showed his subjects against simple rustic settings, or placed them in the context of a time-honored myth, such as a pair of classic goddesses symbolizing the forces of nature *(overleaf)*, the actual renderings of the nudes could be quite suggestive.

This special kind of soft-core, party-line pornography, Nazi propagandists hoped, would help to increase the birth rate and inspire battle-weary fighting men with an implied promise of voluptuous Penelopes awaiting their return from the wars. "Coming from the front," asserted Hitler, "they had a physical need to forget all the filth by admiring beauty of form."

Painter Sepp Hilz, at work in his studio in Bavaria, deftly transforms a pretty model into a painting called "Peasant Venus"—a craftsman-like blending of rural simplicity, ideal racial characteristics and concupiscence.

The symbolic—and chastely sexy—figures of Water and Earth (above) make up the central panel of a 1937 triptych, "The Four Elements" by Hitler's favorite painter, Adolph Ziegler. This painting hung in an honored place over the mantel in the Führer's house in Munich.

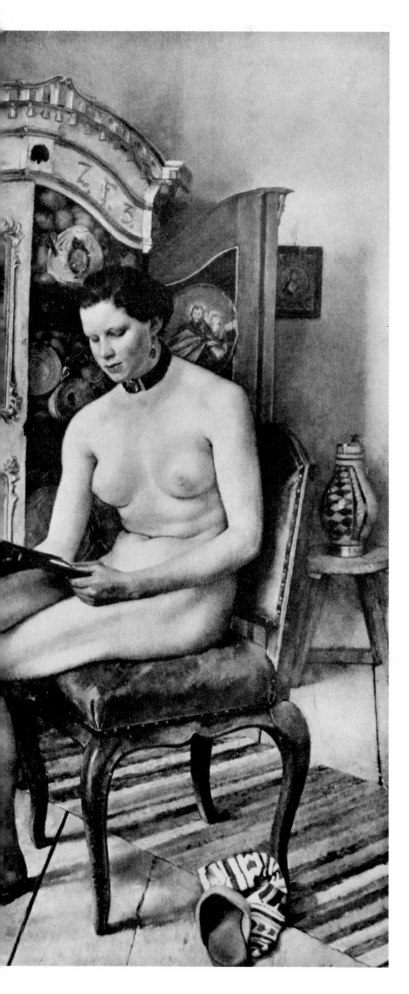

For his 1940 "Vanity," Sepp Hilz used the same model who posed for the "Peasant Venus" (page 175). As with the Venus, he placed her in a farmhouse interior dominated in this oil by an old Bavarian wardrobe.

"Bath in a Mountain Lake," by Julius Engelhard, emphasizes the polished technique and photographic realism characteristic of much Nazi art. For painters of nudes, a healthy, outdoor setting was as safe as allegory or country domesticity for gaining official approval of finished work.

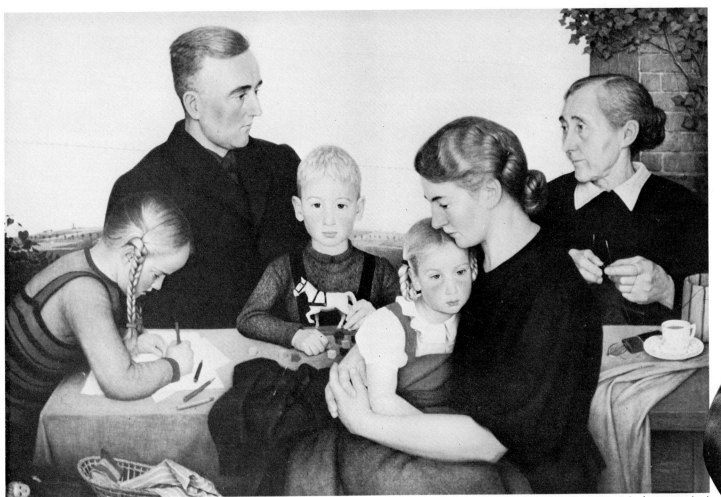

Hitler made much of pictures like Adolf Wissel's "Farm Family," which represented the kind of close, secure home life he espoused—but never had. The father radiates a homespun strength—which his son is beginning to share; the women's downcast or placid eyes suggest secure acquiescence.

Wissel's serene "Locksmith," busy at his bench, portrays the dignity of labor, a recurrent theme in Nazi exhortations to increased productivity.

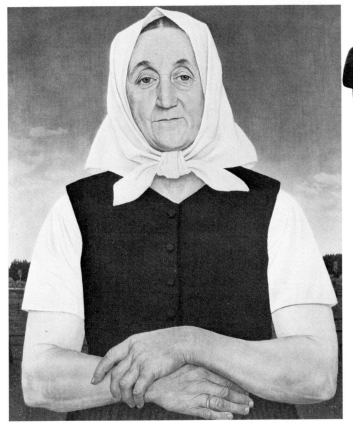

By 1938 when Wissel exhibited "Farm Woman," the Nazis were urging women to replace the men off to the Army in fields and factories.

HUMBLE MEMBERS OF THE MASTER RACE

Hitler's artists not only brought art to the people but also brought ordinary people into art on an unprecedented scale. Hundreds of paintings and statues of the common folk at home or at work reiterated the message that all Germans were really one big hardworking family—united, more than any other people on earth, by blood, soil and steadfast purpose. The subjects of such visual anthems seldom smiled. Jaws, if not actually clenched, were at least firmly set; expressions were sober. Even children and animals seemed imbued with unfrivolous determination or obedience.

Few subjects in these glorifications of labor were ever shown idle. Workers were usually using or at least holding the tools of their trades. Tidy farm people, even when sitting stiffly in their Sunday clothes, somehow gave off the feeling of placid but sturdy readiness for tomorrow's chores. After Nazi art went to war (overleaf), the canonization of farmers and workers continued. In works dedicated to the heroism of Army combatants, stalwarts of labor stood side by side with the troops on acres of canvas and in tons of stone. The implication was clear: workers, too, were soldiers, providing the fighting men with the food and the weapons that were vital to the triumphs of the Reich.

A firm-jawed miner in a 1938 bronze sculpture by Hans Breker, Arno's younger brother, holds his pick much as he might a weapon, to suggest that he is just as important a fighter for the Fatherland as is any uniformed soldier.

The miners above and the farmer at far right are only slightly less prominent than the soldier, the airman and the marine in this 1941 triptych by Hans Schmitz-Wiedenbrück. The civilians actually got top billing in the title: "Workers, Farmers and Soldiers." The servicemen gaze with confidence into the future over the viewer's head; the home-front toilers communicate a quiet pride in supporting the Reich's fighting men by looking directly into the eyes of the spectator.

6

When the French Commander-in-Chief, General Maxime Weygand, set about during the final stages of the battle of Dunkirk to try to organize a new defensive position in northern France, he was faced with a desperate situation. There was little help for France now. The Belgians and the Dutch had been defeated, and the British, but for a few divisions, had been driven from the Continent. The French Army, on which the country's fate depended, had been badly mauled in the fighting in Belgium and northern France, having lost 370,000 dead, wounded or prisoners, three quarters of its medium tanks and most of its motor transport.

Moreover, the morale of the army and of the French nation itself was close to rock bottom. The supposedly invincible Maginot Line, which had been counted upon to keep the German Army out of France forevermore, had proved totally irrelevant to the fighting so far. The Germans had simply outflanked the costly fortifications by attacking through Holland and Belgium. Nothing had availed against the surging panzers, and now they were threatening to swoop down from the north and overrun all of France.

The pessimism that hung over the army and the country as a whole was epitomized by an incident that occurred on the west bank of the Meuse soon after the Germans invaded. In Cernay Wood, the scattered rear guard of France's 21st Foreign Volunteers crouched on the forest floor under a rain of bombs. The bombs were small, but they made a terrifying sound. Hans Habe, a Hungarian journalist who had volunteered for service with the French, recalled later that they "whistled like a hundred sirens."

When the noise subsided, Habe asked the French lieutenant beside him, "Do you think there's still any hope?" The lieutenant looked at Habe as if wondering whether to take him seriously. "Hope?" he echoed. "Maybe a miracle. What else? How would you expect us to win this war?"

As Hitler massed his forces for the decisive blow against France, he was acutely aware that the principal threat to the achievement of his long-range ambitions to dominate all of Europe lay not here but across the Channel. The British Army had slipped from his grasp at Dunkirk. But it had been heavily battered and had lost most of its equipment. The conquest of Britain, therefore, could wait. The priorities had been set seven months earlier, before the invasion of the West was launched. "Our most dangerous enemy is Brit-

THE FALL OF FRANCE

ain," Hitler had declared after the blitzkrieg in Poland, "but we must first beat her continental soldier, France."

Thus in the early days of June the Germans were able to turn their full offensive resources against the hapless French. For that operation, the Germans could call upon approximately 139 divisions. Against this confident, finely honed and battle-tested fighting force, General Weygand was able to muster about 71 French divisions, including the 17 that were still defending the Maginot Line. In addition, he had available two British divisions—the 51st Highland Division and the 1st Armored Division—which had been stranded in France after the evacuation of Dunkirk.

General Weygand chose to make his stand behind the line of the Somme and Aisne rivers stretching southwestward a distance of 225 miles from the English Channel to the northern end of the Maginot Line at Longuyon. Weygand organized a network of hedgehogs—well-dug-in positions, with troops encircling natural tank obstacles such as villages or woods—along the south banks of the rivers. In addition to the hedgehogs were thin infantry reserves and scattered tank units. Beyond these, there were no further defensive positions. General de Gaulle, by this time, had urged Weygand to mass the 1,200 or so tanks he claimed were still left to the French in two great concentrations in the rear so that they could attack the German columns when they broke through. That way, he said, they might have "a battle instead of a débâcle." But Weygand was an old man (73), and though he had served as Chief of Staff to the revered Marshal Foch in World War I, he had never commanded troops in combat, nor made any real effort to absorb the new concepts of mobile, armored warfare. De Gaulle's plea went unheeded.

In addition, even before the battle began the Germans had gained a crucial tactical advantage. As they curled around the Allied forces at Dunkirk, the aggressive panzers had struck left-handedly to seize five bridgeheads across the lower Somme. Determined Anglo-French efforts to wipe out these bridgeheads had failed. And when the final battle began, these advanced German positions were poised like daggers against the heart of France.

As the Wehrmacht faced south, General von Bock's Army Group B was on the right, next to the Channel. It was to jump off on June 5 and drive across the Somme, then race to the Seine. Four days later, Rundstedt's Army Group A —with Guderian's panzers in the vanguard—was to attack east of Paris, drive a wedge between the two French Army groups fighting there and pin one against the back of the Maginot Line, which faced Germany's own Siegfried Line all along the common frontier.

One of Bock's group of armies made its move on the plain of Picardy in the very early morning of the 5th and it ran into heavy French resistance at first. Captain Jungenfeld, who was commanding a tank battalion at Ablaincourt, reported: "In front of us, every village and wood—one might even say every clump of trees—is literally stuffed with guns and defenses; even small artillery detachments can put us under direct fire. Behind us is the glare of a vicious battle where one fights not only for each village, but each house. We are not therefore surprised to find ourselves under fire from all quarters, and one could say: 'Nobody knows which is the front and which is the rear.' " In his diary, Bock also noted that "it seems that we are in trouble."

His gloom was soon to be dispelled by one of the War's most daring and resourceful commanders: Erwin Rommel. While news of stubborn French resistance was reaching Bock's headquarters, Rommel's 7th Panzer Division—called the Ghost Division because of the way it glided through the night to turn up unexpectedly in the enemy's rear—was about to achieve a spectacular coup on the Somme.

On the 7th Panzer's front, the river ran through a marshy stretch that was about a mile wide. This swamp was crossed by two parallel railway bridges which the French had left intact in the hope that they would be able to launch a counterattack in the sector. On the morning of June 5, Rommel's panzer units seized the bridges and, in full view of French troops on an escarpment that overlooked the south bank of the Somme, tore up the rails. Then the tanks and motor transport crossed the narrow rights-of-way under shellfire, an operation that Rommel compared to a combination of walking a tightrope and running the gauntlet. It was an operation that on paper would scarcely have been considered practicable, even as a field exercise, but Rommel's men brought it off masterfully under battlefield conditions. They hammered a fatal wedge into the French front: by nightfall they were eight miles beyond the Somme; by the next morning they were 12 miles farther still, and on the following day

THE GREAT FRAUD OF THE HITLER TWO-STEP

Just after the fall of France, the Western world was confronted in newsreels and still-photo sequences by the vision of an ebullient Hitler dancing what appeared to be a victory jig in the same forest glade at Compiègne where Germany had surrendered in 1918 at the close of World War I. The Führer was pictured with his official photographer Heinrich Hoffmann *(left in frame three)* and other Nazi leaders, accepting the French surrender on June 17.

Lest anyone forget the humiliation of the German dictator merrily dancing on the grave of France, the pictures kept being reshown in American and British movie theaters and periodicals throughout the War. What most people who saw the pictures never knew was that Hitler did not really dance his little jig—what looked to be a series of jubilant hops was actually a clever fraud that was cooked up by an Allied propagandist.

The visual trick was born when the original news film, which had recorded the surrender of the French at Compiègne, reached the London desk of John Grierson, General Manager of Wartime Information for the Dominion of Canada. The film footage included a very brief series of frames that showed Hitler stamping his foot just once *(top row, below)*.

Struck with a cinematographic inspiration, Grierson decided to choreograph this simple movement into a dance by using a film editing technique called looping.

First, the relevant frames of the one-time foot stamp were copied photographically several times; then the copies were spliced together. In the sequence that resulted, Hitler's foot appeared to move up and down several times, as shown in frames 14, 15, 16 and 17 of the extended strip at bottom. This vision of the conqueror looking like a grinning windup toy turned out to be one of the propaganda triumphs of the decade, leaving Allied audiences in a state of suitable fury until both Hitler and his triumph had been buried.

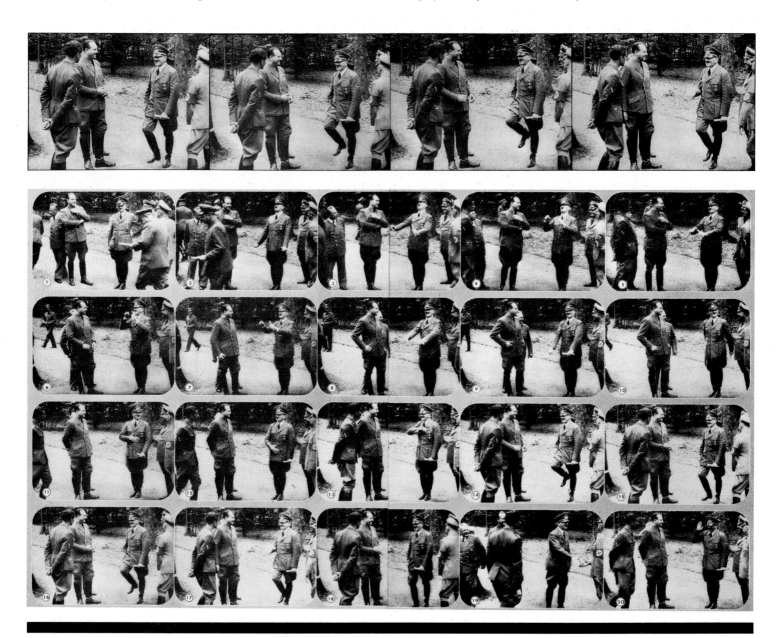

they were driving hard for the Seine. The French front had been torn wide open, never to be sealed again.

In the next few days Bock ordered his troops to turn westward toward the coast, thereby trapping part of the British 51st Division and a sizable French force at the seaport of St.-Valéry-en-Caux. For a time, a miniature Dunkirk appeared to be in the making. On June 10, a Royal Navy flotilla commanded by Admiral Sir William James reconnoitered the coast with a view to evacuating the beleaguered troops, and came under heavy fire from enemy guns near St.-Valéry. Even while James made plans for a night rescue, enemy tanks broke through onto the cliffs and beaches around the harbor. There was still a slim chance of pulling the men out under cover of darkness; but while enemy fire raked the beaches and the harbor, the men waited and the ships tried to maneuver in the dark, a thick fog enveloped St.-Valéry and the rescue fleet could not get into the port. On June 12, the Allied forces surrendered. More than 40,000 prisoners, including 12 generals, went into the German bag.

Devastating though it was, this German drive was not the main punch. That was launched farther to the east on June 9 by Rundstedt's Army Group A, over the terrain—Belleau Wood and Château-Thierry—where American troops had seen action in 1918. French resistance was stubborn and for a day or two it looked as though the Aisne line might hold. German forces gained bridgeheads on the left bank of the Aisne, but soon lost them under heavy counterattack. To the surprise of General Schubert, leading the German XXIII Corps, "the attack ran up against an enemy whose morale was unshaken and who, in a well-arranged position, stood up to our preparatory artillery bombardment with minimal losses. In many places the French marksmen posted in trees kept up their fire until they had exhausted their last cartridge, without heeding the advance of the German forces."

But the German tide rose again and swept over the defenders. On the evening of June 10, Guderian's tanks crossed the Aisne near Rethel. On the 13th they broke through the line at Châlons-sur-Marne; then they drove steadily southward approximately 200 miles to Pontarlier on the Swiss border, cutting off the 17 divisions still locked up in the great concrete fortress of the Maginot Line.

The fate of General Weygand's armies had now been determined. He had no reserves and no real chance of building up another defensive line anywhere in France. The French Army simply came apart. The breakthrough quickly turned into a gigantic rout, with whole armies and mobs of panic-stricken civilians fleeing together.

Hans Habe described the scene. With a bedraggled group of others of his regiment, he was plodding wearily along a road near Commercy, on the Meuse. "All along the road," he recalled, "we encountered floods of civilians. The villages were burning. The cavalrymen tried to race their horses through the towns, but the horses shied and filled the air with their neighing. Rearing horses landed on top of wagons and carts; women screamed, babies were dropped, soldiers fell to the road, unable to go on." Everywhere they heard the same warning: The Germans are coming! But they were always two kilometers ahead or behind or to the right or the left; always near, an unseen menace.

The scenes of desolation and disaster unfolded endlessly. Habe saw dozens of cars, laden with household goods but out of gasoline and abandoned. "In one village," he reported, "a transport lorry had run into a house wall; the dead soldiers hung out like marionettes with no one to guide their strings, or like hanged men that no one had remembered to cut down. The horn had been jammed and blew without interruption, as though the dead driver and his dead passengers were impatient for the stone wall to move aside."

There were fleeting, incongruous moments when the blue sky and the smell of earth reminded Habe it was spring. But the nightmare quickly resumed. "Your eyes turned back to the flood of limping soldiers, trying in vain to look like men in the presence of the fleeing women. You saw children screaming desperately or still as death; officers' cars blowing their strident horns and trying to open a path; bright cavalry uniforms on nervous, weary horses; wagons with their sleeping drivers; cannon without ammunition; the whole disordered funeral procession of a disintegrated army."

They plodded on, the men's feet "bleeding so freely that the blood oozed through their stockings and shoes." German fighters, playing a game of cat-and-mouse, dropped down from time to time to strafe the struggling column—as Habe recalled, "like a gardener spraying a garden with his hose"—leaving the dead and dying in their wake.

The choice left open to the French now, as the catastrophic campaign neared its end, was brutally simple. They could surrender, or salvage what they could of their army and air force and ship it across the Mediterranean to French colonies in North Africa to continue the War from there. Either step was almost too painful to contemplate, but one of them had to be taken. The man who had to make the choice was the French Premier, Paul Reynaud, a scrappy little man whose instinct was to fight to the end. But he was being crushed by the weight of his responsibilities and by the fast-rising pressures all around him for an early capitulation.

His own cabinet was deeply divided. Leading the forces demanding an armistice was the venerable Marshal Pétain, who had been recalled from his post as Ambassador to Madrid on May 18 to become Vice Premier. Reynaud may have thought that in calling the 84-year-old "hero of Verdun" to the government he was inspiring the French to fight to the bitter end, as they had done in the First World War. Pétain himself was under no such illusion. When he paid a last courtesy call on General Franco, he said: "My country has been beaten and I am being called upon to make peace and sign the armistice. . . . This is the result of thirty years of Marxism. I am being called to take the nation in hand."

"Don't go, Marshal," urged Franco, who had known and admired the venerable military leader for many years. "Let those who have lost the war liquidate it, let them sign the armistice."

"Yes, General," answered Pétain, "but my country calls and I owe myself to my country."

For Pétain, as well as for Weygand, there could be no possibility of continued resistance; the entire Allied cause was doomed. The English had scuttled for home, abandoning their commitments, and would not last more than a couple of weeks once France had fallen. "England will have its neck wrung like a chicken," said Weygand. ("Some chicken. Some neck," said Prime Minister Churchill later, after the Battle of Britain had been won.)

There was a diehard faction in the French government, but it was not strong enough to change the course of events. It was led by another survivor of the First World War, Georges Mandel, who had been the right-hand man of Clemenceau when he ruthlessly suppressed defeatism and spurred the French to victory in 1918. Now Minister of the Interior, Mandel was violently opposed to an armistice. More important, in the long run, was a younger man—he was 50, very young to be a French general—Charles de Gaulle, whom Reynaud had appointed Undersecretary of

State for War. For de Gaulle capitulation was unthinkable; there could be no compromise with the enemy. The War had to be carried on wherever possible, and if that meant giving up the French homeland to fight elsewhere, the prospect would have to be faced.

He spent most of his brief 10 days in office shuttling between England—where he tried to arrange an evacuation of French forces to North Africa—and France, where he backed Reynaud's pleas for continued fighting. He also proposed, and Churchill eagerly seconded, the political unification of France and Britain—meant to prevent a separate peace; the plan came to nothing in the face of French resistance.

Reynaud's morale, severely strained by the defeatists, was under attack from another, more intimate, quarter. His mistress, Countess Hélène de Portes, a chattering society lady, nurtured fantasies of running France the way the Marquise de Pompadour, the mistress of Louis XV, had done two centuries before. At times she did indeed seem to think she was running France. The journalist Pierre Lazareff reported calling at the Premier's office to find him laid low with flu and Madame de Portes sitting at his desk. "Surrounded by generals, high officials, members of parliament, civil servants, she was presiding over a meeting. She did most of the talking, speaking sharply and with authority. From time to time she opened a door, and I could hear her saying, 'How are you feeling, Paul? Keep resting. We are carrying on.'"

General Sir Edward Spears, the British liaison officer, was another observer appalled by Hélène de Portes and her intrusions into affairs of state. He reported that the château near Amboise that Reynaud used as his alternate headquarters was "a madhouse, a stage madhouse about which walked sane actors, whilst backstage, supers rehearsed their lunatic parts." Madame de Portes kept popping into meetings to whisper mysterious messages to one participant or another, and Spears was utterly put off by her.

"What a very unattractive woman, I thought, apart from the ugly expression the presence of Englishmen called forth. She was certainly not pretty and quite as certainly untidy, and her voice even in an undertone made one think of a corncrake, a corncrake muffled under an eiderdown."

This strange woman was wholly in favor of early capitulation. The First Secretary of the American Embassy, H. Freeman Matthews, who was in constant touch with Reynaud, says that her role in encouraging the powerful defeatist elements around the Premier was a crucial one. "She spent an hour weeping in my office to get us to urge Reynaud to ask for an armistice. Never once did we see him that Hélène de Portes was not just coming out of or going into his office, and I think his gradual loss of nerve was in large part due to her influence on him."

While these unnerving influences swirled around the unhappy Premier, the tide of disaster swept ever closer to Paris. The Germans were bearing down from two directions, approaching the capital from the west and the east. For weeks the people of Paris had been watching refugees—first the Belgians, then their own countrymen—plod down the boulevards on their way toward the south of France. Now the Parisians themselves began to look toward the south.

Paris had already had a bitter taste of the war. Waves of German bombers had flown over the city on June 3 and 4, dropping an estimated 1,000 bombs. The Citroën works was seriously damaged and set ablaze; glass and debris littered the Avenue de Versailles and the rue Poussin; a concrete shelter, crowded with women and school children, was crushed, its occupants mutilated beyond recognition. Yet there was no panic, only outrage and a sense of unreality—a feeling that such things could not possibly happen.

"Paris was so quiet and beautiful," André Maurois wrote of that period. "Every morning when I opened my window I could see the loveliest of pale blue skies, the trees of the Bois de Boulogne, the Arc de Triomphe and the Fort of Mount Valérien looking in the mist like a Florentine convent. In the garden below, the concierge was watering the begonias of which she was justifiably proud. In the apartment underneath, a workman whistled a military tune as he mended a tap. Nothing had changed. It could not be true that the Germans were getting perilously near Paris."

Indeed, almost no one seemed to believe it. Theatergoers jammed the Comédie Française and the Bouffes to see the new production of *Cyrano de Bergerac* or the latest Cocteau play. In the cafés, entertainers sang the bittersweet *J'attendrai* ("I'll wait for you; day and night, I will always wait, my love."), and the bookstalls on the Left Bank were doing their usual trade. Then on Sunday, June 9, Maurois recalls, "We began to read in the papers and to hear on the

A month after his country's capitulation, France's new Chief of State, Henri Pétain, receives American newsmen at his residence in Vichy, the capital of the nominally independent state (inset) carved out of France by the terms of the Franco-German armistice. The much venerated 84-year-old Pétain, who had been commander of troops at Verdun in World War I, had accepted the leadership of Vichy France with a grandiloquent statement: "I make to France the gift of my person, to mitigate her suffering." To the reporters, however, he confirmed that there would indeed be suffering in store for his defeated nation: the German-imposed division of France into occupied (red stripes on map) and unoccupied territories, he told them with wry sadness, "is a noose around our necks."

radio quite unexpected names of places . . . Mantes . . . Pontoise. Was it possible the Germans were only half an hour from us by car, while we were living and working just as usual? In the Champs Elysées, the terraces of the cafés were full. We had lunch in the open courtyard of one of the big hotels in the Place Vendôme. There were lots of people at the tables. We went to the cinema: it was nearly full. We saw the attack on Narvik and the Paris raid. The tragedy of last week had already become entertainment."

As further news of the German offensive filtered into the city, the sense of unease deepened; Parisians began to pack their bags. British journalist Alexander Werth found Paris still strangely calm, yet changing. "During day numerous luggage-laden cars seen leaving town with passengers having tears in eyes," he cabled his newspaper. "At night streets almost deserted excepting rifled guards outside government buildings and underground stations. Cafés, restaurants close 10:30. At night distant gunfire hearable, also occasional bombs dropping closer by and in night air there's faint sweet scent of resin and burning trees. It may be woods burning somewhere near front."

On June 10 Maurois received a phone call from his friend Roland de Margerie of Reynaud's staff, telling him that Paris would not be defended and urging him to send his wife south. Another Maurois friend, brain surgeon Thierry de Martel, declared that he would kill himself the moment the Germans entered the city. "I cannot go on living. My only son was killed in the last war. Until now I have tried to believe that he died to save France. And now here is France, lost in her turn. Everything I have lived for is going to disappear. I cannot go on."

Taking one of his final strolls through familiar Paris streets, Werth met a woman friend carrying a little valise. She was not yet going anywhere; she was carrying it "just in case." The valise contained her only valuable possessions: a batch of letters from Anatole France, and a copy of a speech that he had given at her wedding.

Late that evening the telephone rang in the home of a Russian emigrée and her parents. The caller was Alexander Kerensky, Premier of Russia's short-lived provisional government in 1917, now warning that Paris was to be declared an open city and urging his friends to leave at once. "What to take?" the young woman pondered. "I spent the whole night cutting photographs out of my thirty or so albums; my father took along the archives of the Russian Medical Society in Paris, of which he was the chairman; mother busied herself with some food, clothing and pillows, even an eiderdown. We took quite a few books—Russian dictionaries, medical texts, first editions of Nabokov and Bunin—a samovar, a little silver."

Early next morning they loaded their venerable 1926 Citroën, a retired taxicab. In the trunk were several cans of gasoline. To the running board they attached a Peugeot bicycle. "Pillows were on the roof and, inside, our beloved dove was chirruping, undisturbed and unruffled in her cage. The concierge came out to say, 'Au revoir,' some tenants waved, and slowly we went away."

The exodus had begun. One by one the stores and restaurants rang down their steel shutters, the cafés took their tables off the sidewalks. Steady files of cars, taxis and trucks, loaded hastily with provisions and homely treasures, made for the few highways to the south that were still open. Behind them trailed a horde of motorcyclists and bicyclists, pedestrians pushing carts heaped with their belongings or their children, together forming a solid mass of forlorn humanity extending for miles down the roads. General Spears, heading for Tours, met "streams of modest cars packed with people" and festooned with "the most extraordinary assortment of belongings, ranging from bird-cages to pots and pans." Two million Parisians inched along the roads. At villages they stopped and waited in endless queues to buy bread, meat and petrol. "Patient, hopeless queues," Spears noted.

Villagers swelled the flood into a tidal wave, fleeing in trucks with squealing pigs, in hearses, in tractors, on horseback and on foot, few knowing where they were heading. Antoine de Saint-Exupéry observed the exodus from the air. "I fly over the black road of interminable treacle that never stops running," he wrote. "Where are they going? They don't know. They are marching toward a ghost terminus which already is no longer an oasis."

The government itself left for Tours on June 10. Even with armed escorts attempting to clear the way, it took from midnight to dawn for some of the limousines to cover the 160 miles from Paris to their destination on the Loire. Behind them, the lifeblood of the French capital drained away.

A smiling Parisian shopkeeper sells models of the Eiffel Tower to German soldiers. Members of the occupying army also clambered up the real Eiffel Tower, snapped pictures of such Parisian landmarks as Notre-Dame and the Arc de Triomphe, and purchased French-German dictionaries. Responding to the influx of new business, restaurants put up signs reading "Ici on parle allemand" (German is spoken here), and opportunistic French prostitutes solicited customers among the Germans by cooing "Mein Süsser"—my sweetheart—at passing soldiers.

June 10 also marked the entrance of another belligerent into the War. Benito Mussolini, with his own lust for conquest, had for some time been in an envious rage because his protégé, Adolf Hitler, was walking off with the glory. As his son-in-law Galeazzo Ciano put it bluntly in his diary, the Italian dictator was now afraid of losing his share of the spoils. Never mind that he had just been told by his chief of war production that the industrial situation of Italy was catastrophic, that even if they melted down every iron fence in Italy they could not keep their steel mills going for more than a few months. Nothing could hold back Mussolini.

Unlike another protégé of his, Francisco Franco, who refused to bring Spain into the War unless he was guaranteed enormous military and economic aid by Hitler, Mussolini jumped in with no guarantees whatever from Hitler and declared war on France and England in a histrionic harangue to a mob of Fascist enthusiasts in the Piazza Venezia in Rome: "This gigantic battle," he declaimed, "is the battle of the poor and numerous peoples against the famishers who keep ferociously to themselves all the riches and all the gold of the earth." In private, he told his intimates in more down-to-earth language that he "needed a few thousand dead in order to take a seat at the peace table."

From the start, his war was a farce, and not the glorious adventure he had dreamed of. Hitler refused to let him use his air force. His army took 10 days to get started. When it finally moved, it was slowed down further by bad weather in the snowy passes over the Alps and could not even dislodge the skeleton garrisons that the French had left to hold their frontier fortifications. Unable to gain any appreciable ground by themselves, the Italians hatched a plan for coming in on the Germans' coattails. Halder sputtered in his diary: "They have approached us with a scheme to transport Italian battalions behind [General Sigmund von] List's front, so as to get them to the area for which they want to make occupation claims. The whole thing is the cheapest kind of fraud. I have made it plain I will not have my name connected with that kind of trickery." The scheme had to be abandoned, but Mussolini did get at least a few of the casualties he thought he needed: 631 men killed, 2,361 wounded. The French defenders lost 79.

The Germans had little interest in the floundering Italians. Their own triumph was virtually unalloyed. There were pockets of French resistance, but for many German soldiers the campaign was a joyride through empty villages.

By now most of France's leaders were reconciled to de-

feat. Churchill flew to Tours on June 11 and vainly urged them to fight for Paris, street by street, as the English were prepared to do in their own cities. "You cannot imagine how a great city like Paris can hold and swallow up enemy effectives. Whole armies can find their graves in it."

"All that makes no sense any longer," replied General Weygand curtly. "Reducing Paris to ashes will make no change in the final result."

On June 11 Paris was declared an open city. American correspondents trying to reach it before the Germans arrived at its gates faced solid columns of refugee cars jamming both sides of the road. The people they saw were demoralized, angry, betrayed. "They have sold us out like rabbits!" a red-bearded soldier yelled. By June 13, Paris was almost empty. Four fifths of its population had fled. Diplomat Robert Murphy took a noon stroll from the American Embassy to the Place de la Concorde and gazed up the Champs Elysées, normally crammed with honking autos and nimble pedestrians. "But now the only living creatures in sight were three abandoned dogs cavorting beneath the large French flags which still hung at each corner of the great concourse."

Not a shot greeted the enemy as they approached the French capital. On the morning of June 14, General von Bock watched German soldiers goose-stepping under the Arc de Triomphe and down the Champs Elysées and then had a hearty breakfast at the Ritz—while gigantic swastika flags were hoisted at the Arc de Triomphe and atop the Eiffel Tower. Maurois' surgeon friend, Thierry de Martel, plunged strychnine into his veins, and died.

Churchill had flown again to Tours on June 13 in a last effort to shore up the flagging French will to resist. So great was the confusion by now that there was no one at the bomb-damaged airport to receive him. He made his way in a borrowed car to a conference at the prefecture, where the French government now had its headquarters. The air was permeated with gloom. With the Germans barely 60 miles away and charging forward almost unhindered, there was little the Allied leaders could do to devise a positive course of action. Matters were not helped by Madame de Portes, who hovered in the hall and sent dire messages into the conference room: "Tell Paul that we must give up. We must make an end of it. There must be an armistice!"

It was decided to send off an appeal for help to President Roosevelt, even though Reynaud and Churchill knew full well that the President could do little without the sanction of Congress. It was further agreed that the 400 German fliers shot down and captured in France, mostly by British fighter planes, would be sent to England to ensure keeping them out of action. (In the general breakdown that followed, this was not done; the German fliers were freed in time to become, as Churchill noted, "available for the Battle of Britain, and we had to shoot them down a second time.") By the end of this unprofitable meeting it was clear to Churchill and his staff that France was truly finished.

On June 14, the day Paris fell, the French government fled to Bordeaux. General Alan Brooke, in command of the remaining British troops in France, went to see General Weygand for orders. According to Brooke, Weygand told him "the French Army had ceased to be able to offer organized resistance and was disintegrating into disconnected groups." Weygand, in his memoirs, denies saying any such thing, but the condition of the army was undeniable. Brooke was shown a map at General Georges's headquarters on which there were numerous "sausage-shaped indentations" in the French line, representing German tank penetrations of up to 100 kilometers. "I asked him what reserves he had and, holding up his hands in a gesture of desperation he replied, 'Absolutely none, not a man, vehicle or gun left.' "

Despite this, Weygand ordered Brooke to organize and hold a 150-kilometer line to defend Brittany—another of de Gaulle's ideas and one which Weygand had at first strongly resisted. Brooke felt that in the prevailing chaos this defense was pure Alice in Wonderland, and that the only way to save the British troops was to get them out of France at once. He was explaining this to London on a very bad telephone connection when suddenly he found Churchill on the line. "You are there to make the French feel that we are supporting them," said the Prime Minister. "You can't make a corpse feel," said the general bluntly, and after much effort finally persuaded Churchill to permit a general evacuation of the troops.

Once again, as at Dunkirk, the British got away by sea in several operations, just in time to avoid capture. The 1st Armored Division, for example, which had seen hard fighting on the Somme, was ordered to head for Cherbourg. Though the highways were a solid mass of disorganized humanity, the British tanks managed to keep moving by avoiding the main roads. In an all-out push, they made 175 miles in 20 hours and reached Cherbourg safe and sound. They did not know it, but they were engaged in a race with General Rommel's 7th Panzer Division, which was also avoiding the main roads. Rommel's unit covered 150 miles in a single day, which it proudly claimed was a record in the history of warfare for an advance through enemy-held territory. Rommel reached the coast on June 18 but was held off until the last of the British steamed out of the harbor late in the afternoon. The city had strong sea defenses with powerful coast artillery, but it was badly equipped for an attack by land. The Admiral of the Port, about to run out of ammunition, ordered its surrender to a vanguard of German tanks, the day after Pétain asked for terms.

On the other side of France, General Wilhelm Ritter von Leeb's Army Group C, which had been defending the Franco-German frontier since the start of the war, now joined the attack and struck at the Maginot Line. Millions of francs

had been spent on sinking tons of concrete into the earth to build the well-equipped, well-ventilated fortresses of the Line, behind which Frenchmen had been taught to feel secure. But all mobile units, desperately needed for counterattack, had been withdrawn to other sectors, and France's last bulwark was pierced within a few hours. The Germans used infantry with minor tank support. Despite claims of the Line's impregnability, it seemed not to have been so well fortified after all. "The French strong points," says General von Mellenthin, who led one of the attacking divisions, "were not proof against shells and bombs, and moreover, a large number of positions had not been sited for all-round defense and were easy to attack from the blind side with grenades and flame-throwers."

This was but one more drop in France's already full cup of despair. Now the whole nation seemed to be turning into an inchoate mass of individuals. The cities and towns had no administrators left and, in many cases, no essential services. Perhaps 10 million people, a quarter of the French population, were wandering more or less aimlessly over the countryside, thinking only of where they could scrounge their next meal and how they could keep out of the way of the German planes cruising overhead. The demoralized columns of the retreating French armies were barely distinguishable from the hordes of civilian refugees occupying the same roads, crossing by the same bridges and searching out the same supplies of food. Units which did try to put up resistance often found themselves blocked not only by the perpetual traffic jam of the refugees but also by the active opposition of civilians who did not want to see valuable property destroyed when the war was lost anyway.

The Germans, trim, fit and superbly disciplined, made a dramatic contrast to the fleeing French soldiers. They were under strict orders to behave themselves, and they did. *Wir sind keine Barbaren*, we are not barbarians, they told civilians in the places they overran. They smiled, they helped old ladies cross the streets. They did no looting—it is true they had no need to: they had plenty of paper marks, which the French had to accept as legal tender and which could be used for buying anything available. The initial astonished reaction of Frenchmen was that the Germans, despite all they had heard, were really quite "correct." So it was with a mixture of relief and shame that the dazed people of France

"To all Frenchmen. France has lost a battle but France has not lost the war!" proclaims this poster, which was excerpted from a speech made by Charles de Gaulle on June 18, 1940, a few days after the fall of France. From a newly set up London headquarters, to which de Gaulle had fled from Bordeaux, he was presiding over a government-in-exile and striving to build an army made up of French troops evacuated from Dunkirk, colonial forces, and French civilians who managed to slip out of France. With these men, who were to be supplied and armed by the British, de Gaulle hoped to reverse the tide of defeat and to reconquer France.

learned on June 17 that their government was ready to surrender. Worn out by the quarrels and intrigues around him in Bordeaux, Paul Reynaud had finally resigned. He was succeeded by Marshal Pétain, who announced to his people with his quavering aged voice: "It is with a heavy heart that I tell you today that we must stop the fighting." After such a statement, few soldiers saw any reason to go on.

The next day another French voice was heard, this one with a message of undefeated hope. General de Gaulle, who had fled to London just in time to avoid being arrested by the new government, made an eloquent radio plea to France to continue the fight. "This War is not limited to the unhappy soil of our country. This War has not been decided by the battle of France. This War is a World War."

There were few to pay attention on that 18th of June. Not many French radios were tuned to London that day; most were trying to get the latest news from Bordeaux. Even in England, few of the French soldiers and sailors awaiting repatriation chose to listen to an obscure general's appeal to go on fighting with their allies.

The world, as well, was interested in more important things than one more refugee general in London. Of prime concern was what terms the Germans would impose on their defeated foe. What, above all, did the victors intend to do about the French fleet, still intact and, suddenly, in the concepts of high strategy of June 1940, perhaps the most critical piece of property in the world? In English hands, the French fleet could help keep Hitler blockaded on the Continent. In German hands, it could help destroy England. Either way it might be decisive to the outcome of the War.

Hitler played a cool hand; he was not going to throw away what he wanted for the sake of personal satisfaction. He was, as Ciano noted in his diary, like a gambler who had won a big pot and now wanted to get out of the game with his winnings intact. To do this, he must avoid imposing such harsh terms on the French that they would be provoked into sailing off for North Africa and continuing the struggle. This meant, among other things, that Mussolini could not, for the moment, get the spoils he had rushed so eagerly into the War to grab. Hitler informed a humiliated (Ciano's word) Duce that he would have to settle for whatever ground his armies had conquered—a few square meters of rock and snow. Mussolini had no choice but to agree, and blamed his failure on his army's lack of modern equipment: "Even Michelangelo," he said, "had to have marble to make statues."

The French plenipotentiaries who were sent through the German lines on June 21 had no idea what terms they would be offered, nor even where they were going. Only after an exhausting 30 hours of travel did they find that Hitler, with his flair for the dramatic, had brought them to the clearing in the forest of Compiègne where Marshal Foch had dictated his armistice terms to the Germans in November 1918. The sleeping car in which the signing of the document had taken place had been put in a special museum by the French. At Hitler's orders, a wall of the museum was knocked down and the car returned to the siding on which it stood in 1918.

Hitler savored every moment of his triumph. It was a hot afternoon when he arrived. He wore his simplest uniform, with the single decoration of the Iron Cross on it—amid his staff bedecked and bespangled with gold braid and medals. He led his party right up to the great granite monument which the French had raised on the spot (and which he was to blow up three days later) with its inscription reading: "Here on the eleventh of November 1918 succumbed the criminal pride of the German Empire—vanquished by the free peoples which it tried to enslave." William L. Shirer, the American radio correspondent, who was standing only a few yards away, saw Hitler's face "afire with scorn, anger, hate, revenge, triumph. He steps off the monument and contrives to make even this gesture a masterpiece of contempt. . . . He glances slowly round the clearing. . . . Suddenly, as though his face were not giving quite complete expression to his feelings, he throws his whole body into harmony with his mood. He swiftly snaps his hands on his hips, arches his shoulders, plants his feet wide apart. It is a magnificent gesture of defiance, of burning contempt for this place and all that it has stood for in the 22 years since it witnessed the humbling of the German Empire."

The terms read out to the French in the sleeping car were, in fact, harsh, but not quite harsh enough to drive them to reject the proposal and continue fighting. Hitler did not insist on the occupation of all French soil; he kept approximately only the regions his armies had already conquered plus a coastal strip running down to Spain. He made no demands, for the moment, on the French overseas empire. The only really odious clause in the armistice was the one binding the French to turn over the anti-Nazi German refugees to whom they had given shelter. When General Charles Huntziger, one of the French delegation, protested this provision, General Keitel told him that "warmongers and traitors" would be extradited "at all costs."

On the all-important question of the fleet, the armistice provided that the French warships were to be disarmed in their home ports under German and Italian supervision; but the Germans and Italians guaranteed not to make use of them in any subsequent hostilities.

For the French, this was hard but not entirely unacceptable. If the Germans tried to seize the ships, their admirals were determined to sink them. But to the British, putting the fleet under German-Italian supervision meant that the ships were being delivered directly into the hands of the enemy, and it was essential—a matter of life and death—for them to prevent any such eventuality.

The official British war history subsequently noted, on the basis of information which later came to light, that both Hitler and the British would probably have accepted a compromise solution calling for the interning of the French fleet in neutral harbors. But no one was aware of this at the time, and the result was bitterly ironic: the last battle of the French campaign would be fought not between the Allies and the Germans but between the Allies themselves.

The British Admiralty was determined to secure or sink every French warship afloat. The French squadrons that had taken shelter in Portsmouth and other English harbors were boarded by assault parties in predawn raids and captured—with little difficulty. In Alexandria, the British and French admirals commanding the ships in the harbor worked out an agreement by which the French vessels would be disarmed and sit out the War where they were. Two new French superbattleships, the *Richelieu* and the *Jean Bart,* whose construction had not quite been completed, had escaped from their Atlantic coast shipyards just ahead of the Germans and reached West African ports, where they were beyond the reach of the British Navy for the moment.

That left the main French battle squadron, at anchor in the base of Mers-el-Kebir near Oran in Algeria. A powerful British naval squadron under Admiral Sir James Somerville steamed up to it on the morning of July 3 and gave a three-choice ultimatum to the French Admiral, Marcel-Bruno Gensoul: He could join the Allies, or sail his ships with reduced crews to be interned in British ports, or sail them to be demilitarized in the West Indies. If he accepted none of these terms, his ships would be blown out of the water.

What followed was an appalling mixup between the British and the French. Both sides made crucial decisions without full possession of the facts. The British were unaware that the French were attempting to negotiate a change in the terms relating to the fleet; in fact, at this point the English had not yet even seen the full text of the Armistice terms.

Admiral Gensoul, on his side, did not radio to his chiefs the full text of the British ultimatum, he said only that he had been offered the choice of surrendering or being sunk. At the last minute Gensoul (who may only have been playing for time) offered to demilitarize his ships where they were. But it was too late; the time limit of the ultimatum had expired at 6 p.m. Somerville—who was personally convinced that his French comrades-in-arms would never permit their ships to fall into German hands and that the whole confrontation was a tragic error—obeyed a direct order from London and opened fire. The French battle cruiser *Strasbourg* and a few destroyers managed to get away to Toulon. But four large warships, trapped in the anchorage, were sunk or disabled, with the loss of 1,267 French lives.

It was hardly a glorious victory, but it was greeted with enthusiasm in England because at least it demonstrated that there was now a government in London that was capable of decisive, even if unpleasant, action. The French quite naturally did not share this enthusiasm; sailors, soldiers and civilians alike were outraged over the British act of aggression. Marshal Pétain's government broke off diplomatic relations with Britain. The Allies who had marched off to war *bras dessus bras dessous* were now as good as enemies. The final irony of the disastrous campaign in the West had been played out, leaving France and Britain embittered and estranged. The bitterness was wryly expressed by Anthony Eden, Britain's Secretary of State for War.

"Why are you in such wonderful spirits today?" King George asked Eden. "Because we are all alone, Sir," Eden replied. "We haven't an ally left."

Britain was indeed alone, and Hitler could now turn his attention to the conquest of that island kingdom.

A DICTATOR'S DREAM TOUR

ADOLF HITLER WITH HIS ESCORT ON THE HEIGHTS OF MONTMARTRE

THE TOURISTS ON THE STEPS OF THE MADELEINE

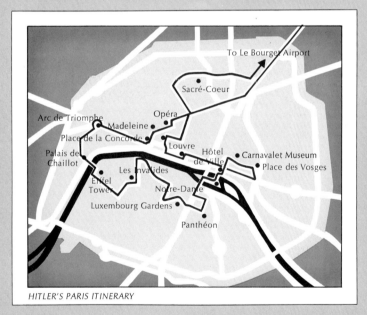

To Le Bourget Airport

Sacré-Coeur

Opéra

Arc de Triomphe
Madeleine
Place de la Concorde
Louvre
Hôtel
de Ville
Carnavalet Museum
Palais de
Chaillot
Les Invalides
Place des Vosges
Eiffel
Tower
Notre-Dame
Luxembourg Gardens
Panthéon

HITLER'S PARIS ITINERARY

THROUGH PARIS AT A GALLOP

The newspaper vendor in the Place de l'Opéra couldn't believe his eyes. There, almost within reach, stood Adolf Hitler, conqueror of France. The German leader was posing for photographs in front of the famous Opéra, behaving like any ordinary sightseer. The time was 6 a.m.; the date June 23, 1940, just one day after the French capitulation.

For Hitler, who had flown in from Belgium, the visit—his first and last—was a dream come true. His yearning to see Paris had begun when, as an art student, he had pored over pictures of the city's historic sites. Now, Paris lay under his victorious hand, all his own to savor as few men had been privileged to do. Oddly, Hitler, with his aides, an armed escort and two artist favorites, architect Albert Speer and sculptor Arno Breker, chose to pack his dream into three pell-mell hours, like a vacationing school teacher on a 10-city package tour.

Speeding through the misty streets of Paris, the party followed the route marked on the map at left. (The high spots, all well known to tourists, are shown on the following pages.) At the Opéra, whose architectural plans he had studied, Hitler led the way. Once he paused and announced a room was missing. Told the chamber had been walled up during an earlier renovation, the Führer said triumphantly: "You see how well I know my way around here!"

From the Opéra, the motorcade went on to the Madeleine, one of the city's numerous memorials to the Napoleonic era, then drove around the Arc de Triomphe and stopped near the Eiffel Tower, where Hitler paused for a travel album snapshot with his artist companions. At Napoleon's Tomb, in the Invalides, the Führer stared at the red porphyry sarcophagus of Europe's last great conqueror, and murmured, "This is the finest moment of my life."

Cursory halts at the Panthéon, the Hôtel de Ville and the church of Sacré-Coeur ended the rapid inspection. Out at Le Bourget airport, surrounded by his admiring troops prior to the trip back to headquarters, the racing Hitler finally relaxed, a soldier among soldiers. Like many another tourist he was glad to be on his way home.

HITLER AND HIS ENTOURAGE APPROACHING THE GRAND STAIRCASE OF THE OPERA

LEAVING THE PLACE DE LA CONCORDE

APPROACHING THE ARC DE TRIOMPHE

WITH ARCHITECT SPEER (LEFT), AND SCULPTOR BREKER BEFORE THE EIFFEL TOWER

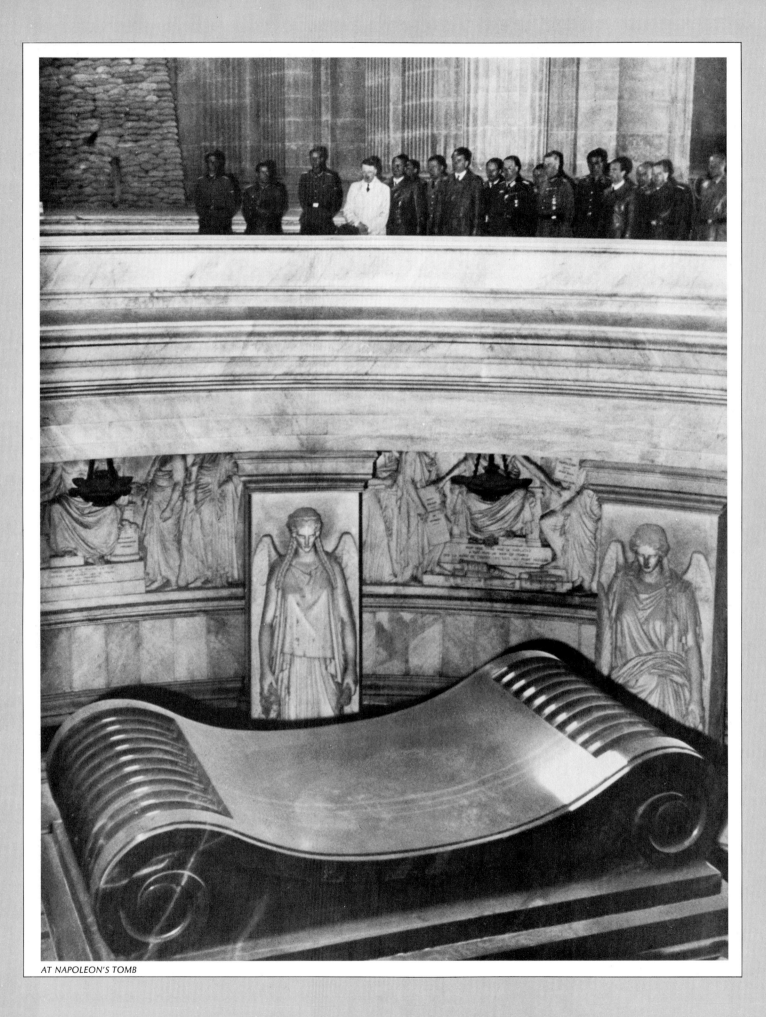

AT NAPOLEON'S TOMB

IN FRONT OF THE INVALIDES

IN THE INVALIDES HONOR COURT

ON THE ESPLANADE AT SACRE-COEUR

BACK AMONG HIS SOLDIERS AT LE BOURGET AIRPORT

BIBLIOGRAPHY

Addington, Larry H., *The Blitzkrieg and the German General Staff 1865-1941*. Rutgers University Press, 1971.

Ansel, Walter, *Hitler Confronts England*. Duke University Press, 1960.

Anders, Wladyslaw, *An Army in Exile*. Macmillan & Co., Ltd., 1949.

Baldwin, Hanson, *Battles Lost and Won*. Harper & Row, Publishers, 1966.

Barber, Noel, *The Week France Fell*. Macmillan London Limited, 1976.

Bauer, Eddy, *Histoire Controversée de la Deuxième Guerre Mondiale, 1939-1945*. Editions Rombaldi, 1966.

The Belgian Campaign and the Surrender of the Belgian Army May 10-28, 1940. Belgian American Educational Foundation, Inc., 1940.

Belgium. Didier Publishers, for the Belgian Ministry of Foreign Affairs, 1942.

Benoist-Méchin, Jacques, *Sixty Days That Shook the West: The Fall of France 1940*, translated from the French by Peter Wiles. G. P. Putnam's Sons, 1963.

Bergschicker, Heinz, *Der Zweite Weltkrieg*. Deutscher Militärverlag (Berlin), 1966.

Bethell, Nicholas, *The War Hitler Won*. Holt, Rinehart and Winston, 1973.

Boveri, Margret, *Treason in the Twentieth Century*, translated from the German by Jonathan Steinberg. G. P. Putnam's Sons, 1963.

Briggs, Susan, *The Home Front*. American Heritage Publishing Co., Inc., 1975.

Brissaud, André, *Canaris*, translated from the French by Ian Colvin. Grosset & Dunlap, 1974.

Bullock, Alan, *Hitler: A Study in Tyranny*. Harper & Row, 1962.

Bryant, Arthur, *The Turn of the Tide*. Doubleday & Company, Inc., 1957.

Butler, J. R. M., *Grand Strategy*, Vol. II. Her Majesty's Stationery Office, 1957.

Calder, Angus, *The People's War*. Pantheon, 1969.

Calvocoressi, Peter, and Guy Wint, *Total War*. Pantheon, 1972.

Chapman, Guy, *Why France Fell*. Holt, Rinehart and Winston, 1968.

Churchill, Winston, *The Gathering Storm*. Houghton Mifflin Company, 1948.

Collier's Photographic History of World War II. P. F. Collier & Son Corp., 1944.

Condon, Richard W., *The Winter War*. Ballantine Books, 1972.

Collier, Basil, *The Second World War: A Military History*. William Morrow & Company, Inc., 1967.

Collier, Richard, *Sands of Dunkirk*. E. P. Dutton and Company, 1961.

Collins, James L., ed., *The Marshall Cavendish Illustrated Encyclopedia of World War II*. Marshall Cavendish Corp., 1972.

Culver, Bruce, *PzKpfw IV in Action*. Squadron-Signal Publications, 1975.

De Gaulle, Charles, *The Complete War Memoirs of Charles de Gaulle*. Simon and Schuster, 1964.

Divine, Arthur D., *The Nine Days of Dunkirk*. Norton, 1959.

Doorman, P. L. G., *Military Operations in the Netherlands*. George Allen and Unwin, Ltd., 1944.

Draper, Theodore, *The Six Weeks' War*. The Viking Press, 1964.

Eden, Anthony, *The Reckoning*. Houghton Mifflin Company, 1965.

Ellis, Chris, Peter Chamberlain and John Batchelor, *German Tanks 1939-45*. Purnell's History of the World Wars Special. Phoebus Publishing Company-BPC Publishing Ltd., 1975.

Ellis, L. F., *The War in France and Flanders; 1939-1940*. Her Majesty's Stationery Office, 1953.

Erickson, John, *The Soviet High Command*. St. Martin's Press, 1962.

Esposito, Brigadier General Vincent J., ed.:
The West Point Atlas of American Wars, Vol. II. Frederick A. Praeger, 1964.
A Concise History of World War II. Frederick A. Praeger, 1964.

Fest, Joachim, *Hitler*, translated from the German by Richard and Clara Winston. Vintage Books, 1975.

Fleming, Donald, and Bernard Bailyn, *The Intellectual Migration*. The Belknap Press of Harvard University Press, 1969.

Fonvieille-Alquier, François, *Les Français dans la Drôle de Guerre*. Editions Robert Laffont (Paris), 1971.

Fuller, J. F. C.:
A Military History of the Western World, Vol. III. Minerva Press, 1956.
The Second World War 1939-45. Meredith Press, 1962.

Galland, Adolf, *The First and the Last*, translated from the German by Mervyn Savill. Henry Holt and Company, 1956.

Gorlitz, Walter, ed., *The Memoirs of Field-Marshal Keitel*, translated from the German by David Irving. Stein and Day, 1966.

Goutard, André, *The Battle of France, 1940*, translated from the French by Captain A. R. P. Burgess. Ives Washburn, Inc., 1959.

Greene, Nathanael, *From Versailles to Vichy*. Thomas Y. Crowell, 1970.

Grunfeld, Frederic, *The Hitler File*. Random House, 1974.

Güderian, Heinz, *Panzer Leader*, translated from the German by Constantine Fitzgibbon. E. P. Dutton and Company, 1952.

Halder, Franz, *Hitler as War Lord*, translated from the German by Paul Findlay. G. P. Putnam's Sons, 1950.

Hambro, Carl J., *I Saw It Happen in Norway*. D. Appleton-Century, 1940.

Hassell, Ulrich von, *The Von Hassell Diaries 1938-1944*. Doubleday and Company, 1947.

Henderson, Harry B., and Herman C. Morris, *War in Our Time*. Doubleday, Doran & Company, 1942.

Higgins, Trumbull, *Hitler and Russia*. The Macmillan Company, 1966.

Hildebrand, Klaus, *The Foreign Policy of the Third Reich*, translated from the German by Anthony Fothergill. University of California Press, 1973.

Hinkel, Hermann, *Zur Funktion des Bildes im Deutschen Faschismus*. Anabas-Verlag Giessen, 1974.

Horne, Alistair, *To Lose a Battle: France 1940*. Little, Brown and Company, 1969.

Hoyt, Edwin P., *The Army without a Country*. The Macmillan Company, 1967.

Irving, David, *The Rise and Fall of the Luftwaffe*. Little, Brown and Company, 1973.

Jacobsen, H. A., and Hans Dollinger, *Der Zweite Weltkrieg*. Vol. I. Verlag Kurt Desch, 1963.

Jacobsen, H. A., and J. Rohwer, eds., *Decisive Battles of World War II: The German View*, translated from the German by Edward Fitzgerald. G. P. Putnam's Sons, 1965.

Jarrett, George B., *Combat Tanks*. Meredith Press, 1969.

Jakobson, Max, *The Diplomacy of the Winter War*. Harvard University Press, 1961.

Johnson, Amanda, *Norway, Her Invasion and Occupation*. Bowen Press, 1948.

Journal de la France: Les Années Quarante. Jules Tallandier (Paris), 1971.

Kennedy, Robert M., *The German Campaign in Poland (1939)*. U.S. Government Printing Office, 1955.

Kesselring, Albert, *Kesselring: A Soldier's Record*. William Morrow & Company, 1954.

Kirk, John, and Robert Young, *Great Weapons of World War II*. Walker and Company, 1961.

Langer, William L., and S. Everett Gleason, *The Challenge to Isolation*, Vol. I. Harper & Row, 1964.

Latreille, André, *La Seconde Guerre Mondiale*. Hachette (Paris), 1966.

Liddell Hart, B. H.:
The German Generals Talk. William Morrow and Company, 1948.
History of the Second World War. G. P. Putnam's Sons, 1970.

Liddell Hart, B. H., ed., *The Other Side of the Hill*. Cassell and Company Ltd., 1951.

MacIntyre, Donald, *Narvik*. W. W. Norton & Company, Inc., 1959.

Macksey, Kenneth John, *Tank Warfare*. Stein and Day, 1971.

Macksey, Kenneth, and John Batchelor, *Tank*. Ballantine Books, 1971.

Mann, Erika and Klaus, *Escape to Life*. Houghton Mifflin Company, 1939.

Manstein, Erich von, *Lost Victories*, edited and translated from the German by Anthony G. Powell. Henry Regnery Company, 1958.

Mason, Herbert Molloy Jr., *The Rise of the Luftwaffe*. The Dial Press, 1973.

Mellenthin, F. W. von, *Panzer Battles*. University of Oklahoma Press, 1956.

Michel, Henri, *The Second World War*, translated from the French by Douglas Parmée. Praeger Publishers, 1975.

Murphy, Robert, *Diplomat Among Warriors*. Doubleday & Company, 1964.

Norwid-Neugebauer, M., *The Defence of Poland: September 1939*. M. I. Kolin Ltd. (London), 1942.

Ogorkiewicz, Richard M., *Armor*. Frederick A. Praeger, 1960.

Perrett, Geoffrey, *Days of Sadness, Years of Triumph*. Coward, McCann & Geoghegan Inc., 1973.

Petrow, Richard, *The Bitter Years*. William Morrow & Company, Inc., 1974.

Prüller, Wilhelm, *Diary of a German Soldier*, edited by H. C. Robbins Landon and Sebastian Leitner, translated from the German by H. C. Robbins Landon. Coward-McCann, Inc., 1963.

Roskill, S. W., *The War at Sea*. Her Majesty's Stationery Office, 1954.

Rowe, Vivian, *The Great Wall of France*. G. P. Putnam's Sons, 1961.

Shirer, William L.:
Collapse of the Third Republic. Pocket Books, 1971.
The Rise and Fall of the Third Reich. Simon and Schuster, 1960.

Slessor, John C., *The Central Blue*. Frederick A. Praeger, 1957.

Snow, C. P.:
Science and Government. Harvard University Press, 1962.
Appendix to Science and Government. Harvard University Press, 1962.

Spears, Edward, *Assignment to Catastrophe*, Vol. II, *The Fall of France*. A. A. Wyn, 1955.

Speer, Albert, *Inside the Third Reich*, translated from the German by Richard and Clara Winston. The Macmillan Company, 1970.

Spielberger, Walter, *Panzerkampfwagen IV. AFV-Weapons Profiles 43*. Profile Publications Ltd., 1972.

Stein, George, *The Waffen SS*. Cornell University Press, 1966.

Strategicus, *A Short History of the Second World War*. Faber and Faber Ltd., 1950.

Tank, Kurt Lothar, *Deutsche Plastik Unserer Zeit*. Raumbild-Verlag Otto Schönstein K.G., 1942.

Tanner, Väinö, *The Winter War*. Stanford Univeristy Press, 1950.

Taylor, A. J. P.:
English History 1914-1945. Oxford University Press, 1965.
The Second World War. G. P. Putnam's Sons, 1975.

Taylor, Telford:
The Breaking Wave. Simon and Schuster, 1967.
The March of Conquest. Simon and Schuster, 1958.

Trevor-Roper, H. R., *Blitzkrieg to Defeat*. Holt, Rinehart and Winston, 1964.

Thompson, Paul W., *Modern Battle*. W. W. Norton & Company, Inc., 1941.

Von der Porten, Edward P., *The German Navy in World War II*. Thomas Y. Crowell, 1969.

Weygand, Maxime, *Recalled to Service*. Doubleday & Company, Inc., 1952.

Van Kleffens, Eelco Nicolaas, *Juggernaut over Holland*. Columbia University Press, 1941.

Whitehouse, Arch, *Tank*. Doubleday & Company, Inc., 1960.

Wuorinen, John H., *Finland and World War II*. Ronald Press, 1948.

ACKNOWLEDGMENTS

The index for this book was prepared by Mel Ingber. For help given in the preparation of this book the editors wish to express their gratitude to Peter Anderson, New York; Leo Baeck Institute, Inc., New York; Lieselotte Bandelow, Head, Ullstein Bilderdienst, Berlin; Michael Budny, Executive Director, Zarema Bau, Professor Waclaw Jedrzejewicz, Professor Aleksander Korczynski, Dr. Anna Mars, Pilsudski Institute of America, New York; Dr. George Bussmann, Director, Frankfurter Kunstverein, Frankfurt; Jerry L. Campbell, President, Squadron/Signal, Warren, Michigan; Huguette Chalufour, Editions Jules Taillandier, Paris; Cécile Coutin, Curator, Musée des Deux Guerres Mondiales, Paris; Department of Photography, Imperial War Museum, London; Martin Duberman, Distinguished Service Professor of History, Lehman College, City University of New York, New York; Yan Fromerich-Bonéfant, Cabinet des Estampes, Bibliothèque Nationale, Paris; Annette Riley Fry, New York; Dr. Matthias Haupt, Director, Photo Archive Bundesarchiv, Koblenz; Professor Dr. Herman Hinkel, Justus Liebig-Universität Giessen, Giessen; Heinrich Hoffmann, Hamburg; Dr. Roland Klemig, Director, Bildarchiv Preussischer Kulturbesitz, Berlin; Vera Kovarsky, Purdy Station, New York; Colonel Jean Martel, Curator, Musée de l'Armée, Paris; Michael A. Peszke, M.D., University of Connecticut, Farmington; Polish Army Veterans Association of America, New York; Polish Veterans of World War II, New York; John Radziewicz, Boston; Jurgen Runzheimer, Gladenbach; Charles Silver, Film Department, Museum of Modern Art, New York; Richard Taylor, Researcher, United Press International, New York; Harry A. Turton, Manager, Media Relations, General Motors Corporation, New York; Yivo Institute for Jewish Research, New York.

PICTURE CREDITS *Credits from left to right are separated by semicolons, from top to bottom by dashes.*

INDEX

Numerals in italics indicate an illustration of the subject mentioned.

Printed in U.S.A.